Teach Yourself
VISUALLY™

Guitar

Teach Yourself VISUALLY™

Guitar

Visual

by Charles Kim

WILEY

Wiley Publishing, Inc.

Teach Yourself VISUALLY™ Guitar

Copyright © 2006 by Wiley Publishing, Inc., Hoboken, New Jersey. All rights reserved.

Published by Wiley Publishing, Inc., Hoboken, New Jersey

No part of this publication may be reproduced, stored in a retrieval system or transmitted in any form or by any means, electronic, mechanical, photocopying, recording, scanning or otherwise, except as permitted under Sections 107 or 108 of the 1976 United States Copyright Act, without either the prior written permission of the Publisher, or authorization through payment of the appropriate per-copy fee to the Copyright Clearance Center, 222 Rosewood Drive, Danvers, MA 01923, (978) 750-8400, fax (978) 646-8600, or on the web at www.copyright.com. Requests to the Publisher for permission should be addressed to the Legal Department, Wiley Publishing, Inc., 10475 Crosspoint Blvd., Indianapolis, IN 46256, (317) 572-3447, fax (317) 572-4355, or online at http://www.wiley.com/go/permissions.

Wiley, the Wiley Publishing logo, Teach Yourself VISUALLY, and related trademarks are trademarks or registered trademarks of John Wiley & Sons, Inc. and/or its affiliates. All other trademarks are the property of their respective owners. Wiley Publishing, Inc. is not associated with any product or vendor mentioned in this book.

The publisher and the author make no representations or warranties with respect to the accuracy or completeness of the contents of this work and specifically disclaim all warranties, including without limitation warranties of fitness for a particular purpose. No warranty may be created or extended by sales or promotional materials. The advice and strategies contained herein may not be suitable for every situation. This work is sold with the understanding that the publisher is not engaged in rendering legal, accounting, or other professional services. If professional assistance is required, the services of a competent professional person should be sought. Neither the publisher nor the author shall be liable for damages arising here from. The fact that an organization or Website is referred to in this work as a citation and/or a potential source of further information does not mean that the author or the publisher endorses the information the organization or Website may provide or recommendations it may make. Further, readers should be aware that Internet Websites listed in this work may have changed or disappeared between when this work was written and when it is read.

For general information on our other products and services or to obtain technical support please contact our Customer Care Department within the U.S. at (800) 762-2974, outside the U.S. at (317) 572-3993 or fax (317) 572-4002.

Wiley also publishes its books in a variety of electronic formats. Some content that appears in print may not be available in electronic books. For more information about Wiley products, please visit our web site at www.wiley.com.

Library of Congress Control Number: 2005923414

ISBN-13: 978-0-7645-9642-1
ISBN-10: 0-7645-9642-X

Printed in the United States of America

10 9 8 7 6 5 4 3 2 1

Book production by Wiley Publishing, Inc. Composition Services

Praise for the Teach Yourself VISUALLY Series

I just had to let you and your company know how great I think your books are. I just purchased my third Visual book (my first two are dog-eared now!) and, once again, your product has surpassed my expectations. The expertise, thought, and effort that go into each book are obvious, and I sincerely appreciate your efforts. Keep up the wonderful work!

—Tracey Moore (Memphis, TN)

I have several books from the Visual series and have always found them to be valuable resources.

—Stephen P. Miller (Ballston Spa, NY)

Thank you for the wonderful books you produce. It wasn't until I was an adult that I discovered how I learn—visually. Although a few publishers out there claim to present the material visually, nothing compares to Visual books. I love the simple layout. Everything is easy to follow. And I understand the material! You really know the way I think and learn. Thanks so much!

—Stacey Han (Avondale, AZ)

Like a lot of other people, I understand things best when I see them visually. Your books really make learning easy and life more fun.

—John T. Frey (Cadillac, MI)

I am an avid fan of your Visual books. If I need to learn anything, I just buy one of your books and learn the topic in no time. Wonders! I have even trained my friends to give me Visual books as gifts.

—Illona Bergstrom (Aventura, FL)

I write to extend my thanks and appreciation for your books. They are clear, easy to follow, and straight to the point. Keep up the good work! I bought several of your books and they are just right! No regrets! I will always buy your books because they are the best.

—Seward Kollie (Dakar, Senegal)

Credits

Acquisitions Editor
Pam Mourouzis

Project Editor
Suzanne Snyder

Copy Editor
Lynn Northrup

Technical Editor
Adam Stambaugh

Editorial Manager
Christina Stambaugh

Publisher
Cindy Kitchel

Vice President and Executive Publisher
Kathy Nebenhaus

Interior Design
Elizabeth Brooks
Kathie Rickard

Cover Design
José Almaguer

Cover and Interior Photography
Matt Bowen

Special Thanks...

To the following companies for granting us permission to show photographs of their equipment:

- Reno's Music (www.guitarhotline.com)
- Sweetwater
- Ernie Ball, Inc.
- Fender Musical Instruments Corporation
- Gibson Guitar Corp.
- J. D'Addario & Co. Inc.
- Mackie Designs, Inc.
- The Martin Guitar Co.
- Marshall Amplification
- Roland Corporation, U.S.

About the Author

Charles Kim (Chicago, IL) plays guitar, electric and upright bass, pedal steel, banjo, violin, alto saxophone, piano, keyboards, and drums. He teaches guitar, bass, songwriting, recording, and music theory at Chicago's renowned Old Town School of Folk Music. A multifaceted musician, producer, and composer featured on numerous albums, Kim is also a composer and sound designer for film, TV, dance, and theatre companies. His scores have been commissioned and featured by the Royal Academy of Art, Showtime, and the History Channel.

Acknowledgments

I would like to sincerely thank my editors Pam Mourouzis and Suzanne Snyder for giving me the opportunity to write this book. Audrey Cho was kind enough to take my photo. I'd also like to thank my family, friends, bandmates, and the Old Town School of Folk Music, who supported me to grow as a musician.

This book is dedicated to my mother, Hai Ja Kim, who was my first music teacher.

Table of Contents

chapter 3 Tuning the Guitar

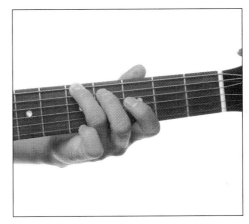

chapter 4 Getting Into Position

chapter 5 Your First Chords

chapter 6 Moving Between Chords

chapter 8 **Rhythm Guitar**

chapter **9** The Rest of the Open Chords

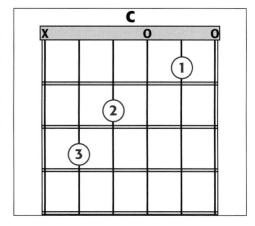

chapter **10** How to Read Chord Symbols, Tablature, and Lead Sheets

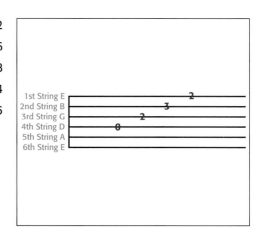

chapter 11 Suspensions and Bass Runs

chapter 12 The Capo and Barre Chords

chapter 13   Chord Progressions

chapter 14   An Introduction to Soloing and Improvisation

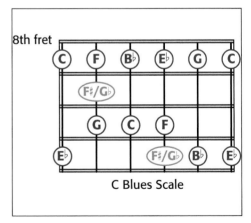

8th fret

C   F   B♭   E♭   G   C

F♯/G♭

G   C   F

E♭   F♯/G♭   B♭   E♭

C Blues Scale

chapter 15 Advanced Techniques

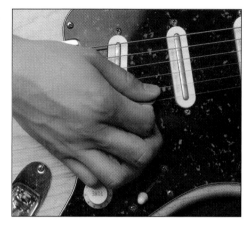

chapter 16 Purchasing and Maintaining Equipment

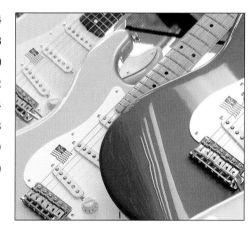

chapter 17 **Electric Guitar Sounds**

Controls on Your Electric Guitar 234
Controls on Your Amplifier 236
Effect Pedals 238

chapter 18 **Continuing Your Guitar Education**

Use a Private Teacher 242
Why Study Music Theory? 243
Learn from Other Guitarists 244
Some Final Advice 245

chapter 1

Introduction to the Guitar and Learning to Play

You've chosen to start off on a musical adventure: playing the guitar. Let's take a look at some of the facets of the instrument and the different musical options it offers.

The Versatility of the Guitar

The guitar is found everywhere in modern popular music. Learning the fundamentals of the guitar unlocks the potential of playing numerous genres of music.

The guitar is found in many genres of music, including folk, classical, rock, pop, blues, country, and jazz. A guitarist can play a melody as well as play chords and accompany a singer. Even a beginning guitarist can embrace all the aspects of a song by playing a few chords while singing the melody.

The guitar is also versatile because it's a remarkably rhythmic instrument. While the guitarist's one hand works the neck of the guitar to create chords and melodies, the other hand works the strings like a snare drum, creating beats and rhythms with fingers or picks. With the power to manipulate harmony and rhythm at the same time, you'll soon realize why it's a primary tool of singers and songwriters.

It's Portable and Affordable

The guitar is an ideal instrument to pick up for many reasons. It's compact and portable, making it easy to take along when meeting with friends for a jam. Beethoven likened it to a miniature orchestra that you could carry in your lap. A good-sounding guitar is also relatively affordable compared to many other instruments.

You'll be playing in just a few pages! Compared to other instruments, the guitar is an instrument you can play from the first day using a few simple chords.

Start Playing Today

Violin and trumpet students have to practice diligently for years to play a major scale with a warm tone while playing in tune. While the guitar will eventually make its intricacies known to you, you can learn the first three chords (see Chapter 5, "Your First Chords") and a simple strumming pattern (see Chapter 8, "Rhythm Guitar") on your first day. The frets, which divide the string length, do the job of keeping you in tune, and you'll play simple rhythms until you develop more coordination. While there are obviously different levels of proficiency you'll eventually want to master, you can start creating music right away!

Set Goals for Yourself

The trick to teaching yourself anything is to practice on a steady schedule and to set realistic goals for yourself. Give yourself time to learn and don't get discouraged if things don't come to you immediately.

Set Realistic Goals

People often become their own worst enemies in learning a musical instrument because they set unrealistic goals. Remember that mastering an instrument involves a learning process that is both mental and physical.

Don't get frustrated: You understand what you have to do, but your hands take time to train. Allow your body to develop muscle strength and memory, which are slower to develop in an adult. You will, however, eventually develop those skills, so don't lose patience!

How to Practice

Develop a reasonable but steady practice regimen. Try to practice every day, if only for 15 or 20 minutes. If you can't practice every day, try not to put your guitar away for several days in a row. Make sure you're playing at least every other day. Leave the guitar next to the TV or somewhere else where you'll see it often, and let your hands get used to the instrument in your spare time.

Starting and stopping your guitar playing will only make the process more discouraging. You will probably progress more quickly than you realize or give yourself credit for. Be prepared to work through the rough spots. Your efforts eventually will be rewarded!

Keep the learning experience fun by playing songs you love. Doing so will take the "work" element out of practicing, and you'll master the skills you need before you know it!

TIP

Learn a song that you love and practice will never be work.

Parts of the Guitar

All guitars have similar essential features, though other features can vary. Before you start playing, let's take a look at the different parts of the electric and acoustic guitar.

Parts of the Acoustic Guitar

Let's get acquainted with the most common parts of the acoustic guitar.

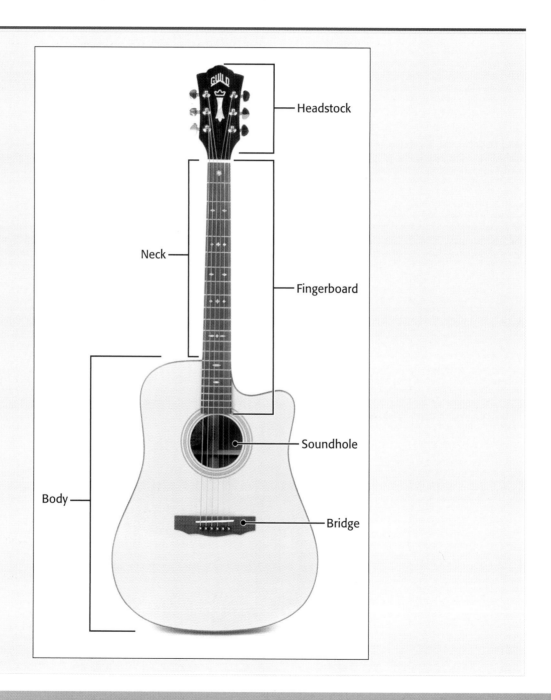

Now let's look at the parts of the electric guitar, some of which are similar to the acoustic guitar, while other components—especially those involving electronics—are different.

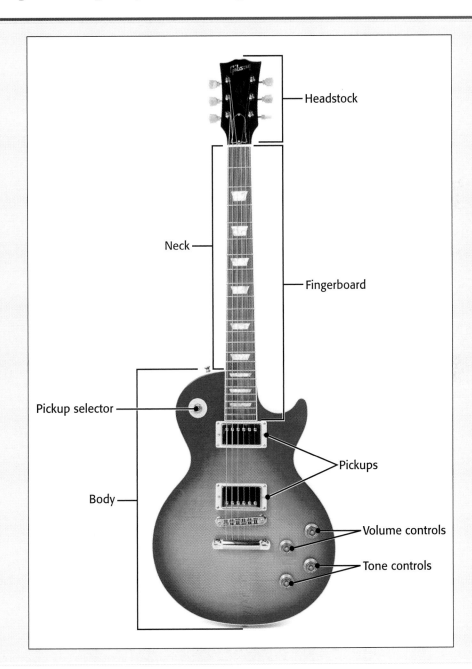

Headstock

Neck

Fingerboard

Pickup selector

Pickups

Body

Volume controls

Tone controls

I'll now describe the parts of both acoustic and electric guitars in more detail, starting with the top of the instrument, the headstock, which contains the tuners.

HEADSTOCK

The headstock is where the strings end at the tuning pegs.

TUNING PEGS

The tuning pegs or tuners tighten or loosen the tension of the strings, thus raising or lowering the pitch of the strings. You adjust the tuning pegs to keep the guitar in tune. Most acoustic guitars, steel-string and nylon, and some electric guitars, have three tuners on the top and three on the bottom of the headstock.

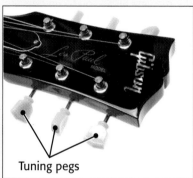

Tuning pegs

TUNING PEG 6–ARRANGEMENT

Some electric guitars have their tuners all along the top, six in a row.

Note: *Remember to keep your string windings neat when you restring your guitar. A crooked string winding will resettle while you play, throwing your string out of tune. For more on restringing your guitar, see Chapter 16, "Purchasing and Maintaining Equipment."*

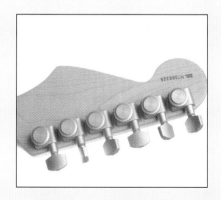

The neck is where guitarists place their fretting hand. For right-handed players, the fretting hand will be their left hand, and vice versa. The fretting hand fingers press on top of the strings, while the thumb provides support on the back of the neck.

FINGERBOARD

The fingerboard is the playing surface of the neck, which is divided by the guitar's frets and stretches down to the body of the guitar.

Fingerboard

MARKERS

The markers allow you to quickly find a specific fret. Some are simple dots, others have ornate inlays. Most manufacturers of steel-string and electric guitars place markers at the 3rd, 5th, 7th, 9th, 12th, and 15th frets.

Markers

SIDE MARKERS

Many guitars have side markers in addition to fingerboard markers, as shown. Classical and other nylon-string guitars usually have markers only on the side of the neck, and not on the fingerboard itself.

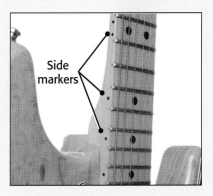

Side markers

CONTINUED ON NEXT PAGE

NUT

The nut stops the vibration on one side of the string (the bridge works on the other side). Nuts can be made of bone, plastic, brass, or other compound material.

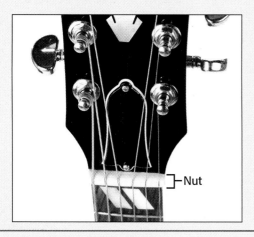

FRETS

The frets are thin strips that run perpendicular to the strings. You place your fingers down on the strings behind the frets, which change the pitch by shortening the strings' length.

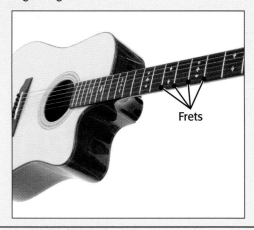

TRUSS ROD

Because of string tension and how wood bends with temperature and humidity changes, many guitars have a truss rod—a metal bar that helps straighten or curve the neck angle. You can find it at the top or the base of the neck. Nylon-string guitars do not have a truss rod.

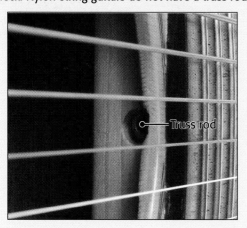

HEEL

The heel is where the back of the neck joins the body of the guitar. It can be plain or elaborate, depending on the style of the guitar.

The body of the guitar houses the rest of the guitar's components. On acoustic and hollow or semi-hollow electric guitars, the body shape, composition, and wood type heavily influence the sound of the guitar. In electric guitars with solid bodies, the body plays a slightly less important role.

The steel string guitar body usually has a soundhole, which allows the guitar to resonate. The bridge holds the strings in place by the use of bridge pins.

Solid-body guitars are the most common electric guitars today. Some guitars, like the Gibson SG and the Telecaster, have bodies that are made of one piece of carved wood.

CONTINUED ON NEXT PAGE

ROUND SOUNDHOLE

The soundhole allows the sound of the guitar to breathe and project. Some guitars have round or oval soundholes.

Round soundhole

F-SHAPED SOUNDHOLE

Early models, especially hollow and semi-hollow guitars, have f-shaped soundholes similar to those found in a violin or cello.

F-shaped soundholes

PICK GUARD

The pick guard's function is to ensure that pick strokes don't scratch the surface of the wood.

Pick guard

END PIN

There is usually a button at the end pin around which you can attach a strap. For more about playing with a strap, see Chapter 4, "Getting Into Position."

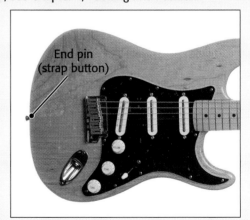

End pin (strap button)

The bridge anchors the strings to the body of the guitar. There are a variety of bridge styles depending on the type of guitar.

STEEL-STRING BRIDGE

On a steel-string guitar, the strings are fastened by bridge pins to a wooden bridge. The pins remain fastened from the tension of the string.

Bridge pin

TELECASTER BRIDGE

In solid-body guitars, such as the Fender Telecaster, the string is more likely to pass through a solid block of metal, which allows the string to ring longer.

LES PAUL BRIDGE

The Les Paul Bridge has a tailpiece where the strings end, and a set of six adjustable saddles which can be fine-tuned for intonation.

CONTINUED ON NEXT PAGE

STRATOCASTER BRIDGE

Some guitar bridges actually move by depressing a vibrato bar. These bridges are suspended between springs with adjustable tension and a set of screws that act as a fulcrum. This is a photo of a Stratocaster bridge.

FLOYD ROSE BRIDGE

This is a photo of a Floyd Rose bridge, which is also of the suspension type.

There are other styles of bridges you should know about as well. On a nylon-string guitar, the string is wrapped and tied around holes drilled through the bridge.

Certain steel-string and electric semi-hollow or hollow-body guitars use a trapeze-style bridge, in which the string is suspended over a wooden bridge, while the ball ends of the string are connected to a metal tailpiece at the end of the guitar.

Depending on the type of guitar you are playing, you will use either nylon or steel strings.

STEEL STRINGS

Steel strings are used on acoustic and electric guitars for country, rock, pop, blues, and slide playing. They have a brighter sound than nylon strings, and have more tension.

The two highest-pitched strings (B and High E) usually are plain steel, while the others are wrapped. The steel itself can be made of phosphor bronze, nickel, or stainless steel.

NYLON STRINGS

Nylon strings are used in classical, flamenco, and certain folk guitars. Traditionally, these strings were made from animal gut. They have a warmer and darker sound than steel strings.

Nylon strings also feel softer to the touch and need less tension to achieve their pitch. The three highest-pitched strings (G, B, and High E) usually are plain nylon, while the Low E, A, and D strings are wrapped with another winding of nylon.

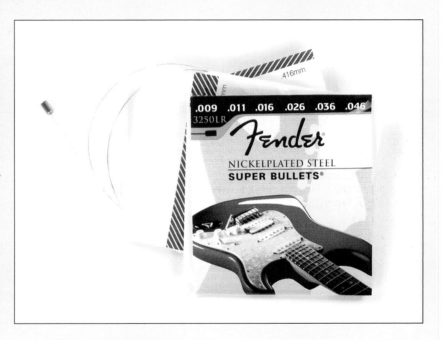

Electric Guitar Controls

Electric guitars are played in the same way as acoustic guitars, but their sound can be radically different. Because of their increased capacity for amplification, sustaining power, tonal variety, and sound manipulation, electric guitars are versatile instruments for sonic experimentation and enhanced rhythms and melodies.

Pickups

SINGLE-COIL PICKUP

The pickups are the microphonic elements that transfer the sound of the strings to the electronic output in an electric guitar. The most common types of pickups are the single-coil pickup and the humbucker pickup. The single-coil has a clear, bright sound.

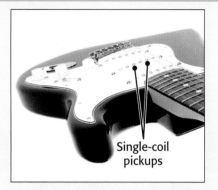

Single-coil pickups

HUMBUCKER PICKUP

In relation to the single-coil pickup, the humbucker pickup has a deep, dark sound.

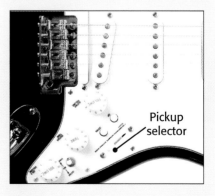

Humbucker pickups

SELECTOR SWITCH

The closer the pickup is to the bridge, the more treble the pickup has. A selector switch is used to select which pickup or combination of pickups is used.

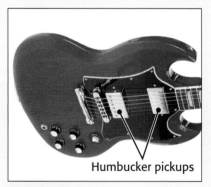

Pickup selector

SINGLE VOLUME CONTROL

The volume control regulates how loud or soft the guitar is. Some guitars, like the Telecaster, have one volume control.

Volume control

LES PAUL VOLUME CONTROL

Other guitars, like the Les Paul, have a volume control that individually controls each pickup.

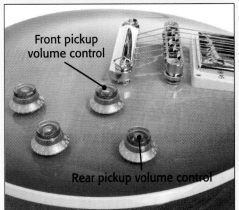

Front pickup volume control

Rear pickup volume control

CONTINUED ON NEXT PAGE

Tone Controls

The tone controls determine how much treble is removed from a pickup's sound, making the guitar sound "bassier."

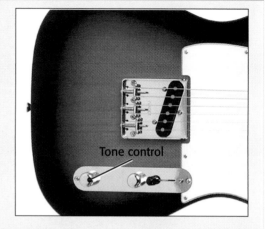

Tone control

Some guitars, like the Telecaster, have one tone control. Others, like the Les Paul, have a tone control that individually controls each pickup.

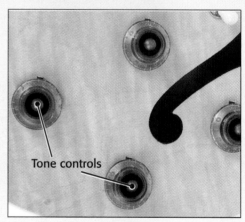

Tone controls

Output Jack

One end of the patch cord is placed in the output jack, while the other is placed in the amplifier to complete the audio path for the guitar's sound.

Output jack

TIP

Be careful with a loose jack. Twisting a cable in a loose jack could cause internal wires to twist and eventually break.

chapter

3

Tuning the Guitar

Before you start playing, let's learn how to get the guitar in tune. You'll learn how to tune both with an electronic tuner and with your ears, using a method called relative tuning.

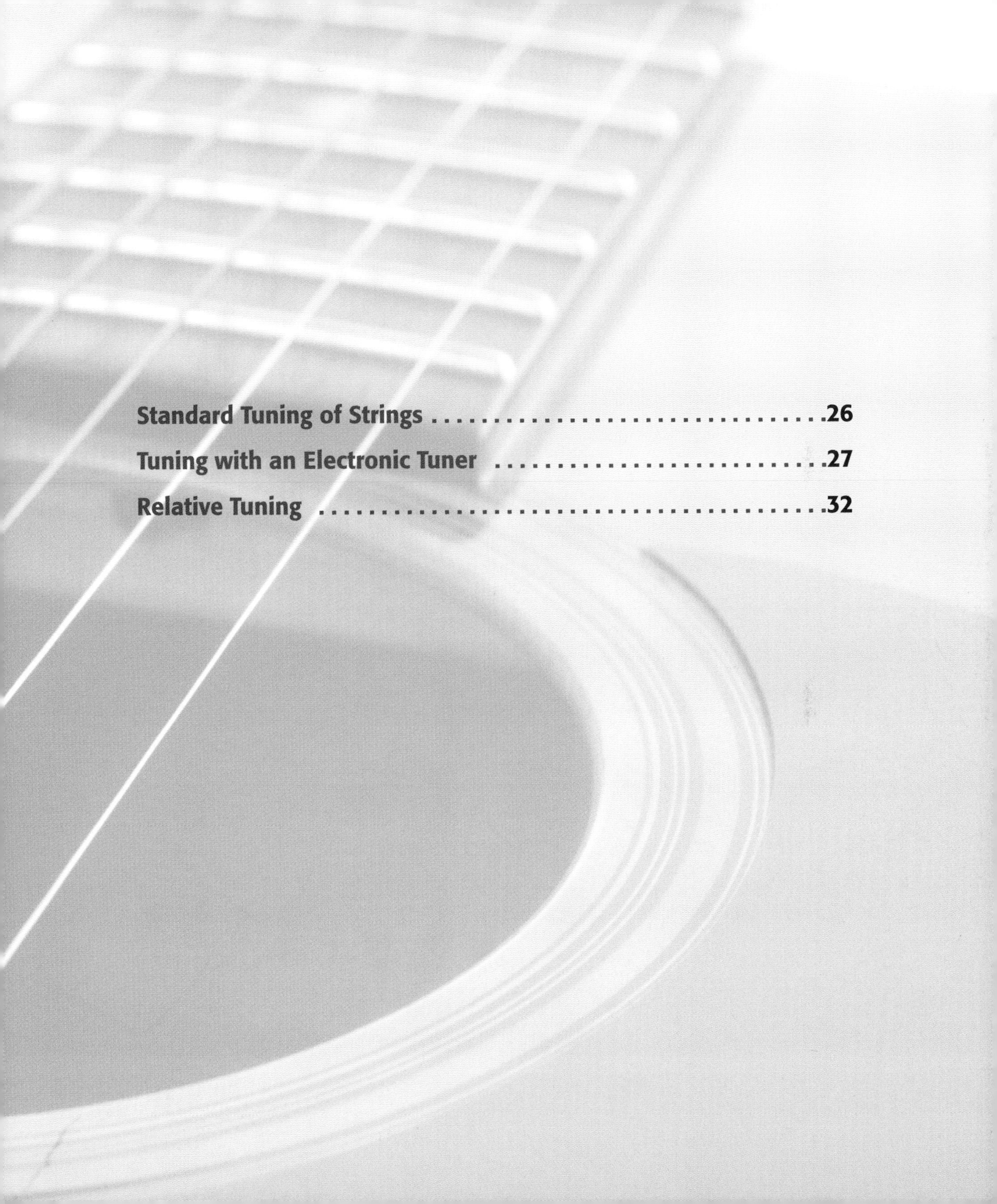

Before we start playing, let's make sure your guitar is in tune, so all the chords sound musically correct. The guitar's standard tuning, from 6th string to 1st string, is E A D G B E.

These are the notes (in the order of fattest string to thinnest) that the open strings on the guitar need to be tuned to. The 6th string is the fattest string, which will be the closest to your head as you hold the guitar. The 1st string is the thinnest string, which will be the closest to your feet.

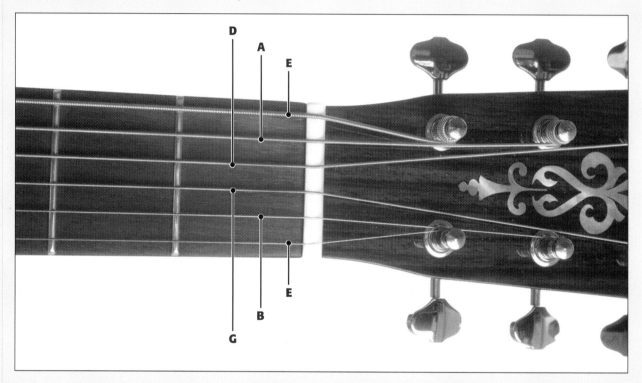

We'll start you tuning with an electronic tuner so you can begin playing as soon as possible. You'll learn about how the different strings are tuned and the scale you need to be aware of when you're tuning.

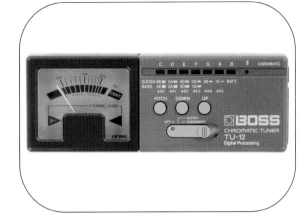

Chromatic Tuner and Chromatic Scale

You should purchase a small electronic chromatic tuner to tune your guitar, as opposed to just a guitar or bass tuner. This way, even if your string is tuned to the wrong note, you can figure out which way you need to tune to correct the problem. Note that the term "tuner" in this sense is different than the physical tuners (tuning pegs) on the guitar's neck that you turn to change a string's pitch (see Chapter 2).

						Chromatic Scale						
C	C#/Db	D	D#/Eb	E	F	F#/Gb	G	G#/Ab	A	A#/Bb	B	C

◄——— Lower ——————————————— Pitch ————————————— Higher ———►

A chromatic tuner will tell you where the pitch of a string is on the chromatic scale. The chromatic scale is all the possible notes in the western musical scale: C-C#/Db-D-D#/Eb-E-F-F#/Gb-G-G#/Ab-A-A#/Bb-B-C

Note: *The notes of C# and Db are called enharmonic notes (a subject that will be discussed in greater length in Chapter 12). They are the same pitch, but have two potential names. The same applies for D# and Eb, F# and Gb, G# and Ab, and A# and Bb. Your tuner may only list the notes by their sharp names or their flat names.*

CONTINUED ON NEXT PAGE

Tune the Low E String

Let's tune the Low E string first. Place the guitar a couple of inches away from the electronic tuner once you've turned it on.

Note: *It is not unusual for the guitar to become extremely out of tune if it hasn't been played for a day, or was bumped in transport.*

You may wish to cover the strings you are not tuning, so the tuner won't get confused by extra ringing strings. You can do this using the palm of your picking hand.

First, pluck the Low E string and make sure that the string is roughly in the vicinity of "E", and not on a different chromatic pitch. Your electronic tuner has an indicator that will show what general chromatic pitch you're on.

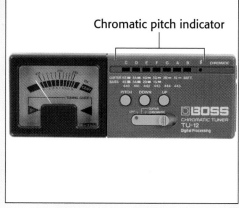

Chromatic pitch indicator

If the electronic tuner reads E, you're ready to fine tune your string. If it reads C, C♯/D♭, D, or D♯/E♭, then your string is *flat* and the pitch is too low. The string needs to be tightened by turning the tuning peg counterclockwise and raising the pitch until you reach the vicinity of E.

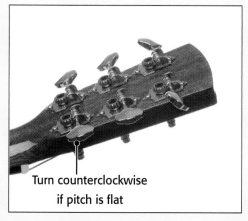

Turn counterclockwise
if pitch is flat

If your E string reads F, F♯/G♭, or G then your string is *sharp* and the pitch is too high. The string needs to be loosened by turning the tuning peg clockwise until you reach the vicinity of E.

Note: *On some guitars the tuners are reversed so that the low E tuning peg is on the bottom of the headstock. If you play one of these guitars in which the tuners are reversed, know that you'll need to turn the tuning pegs clockwise to raise the pitch and counterclockwise to lower it.*

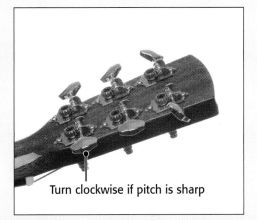

Turn clockwise if pitch is sharp

FINE TUNING

Once you've got the note of E in your chromatic indicator window, you need to fine-tune it exactly to E. Look at the window with the digital 'needle' indicator.

If the indicator is on the left side of the center line, the note is flat. Turn the tuning peg counterclockwise to raise the pitch.

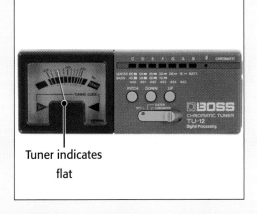

Tuner indicates
flat

If the indicator is on the right side of the center line, the note is sharp. Turn the tuning peg clockwise to lower the pitch.

CONTINUED ON NEXT PAGE

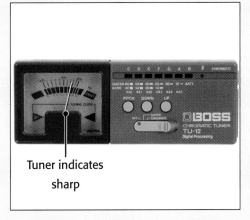

Tuner indicates
sharp

Once you've got both "E" in the chromatic pitch window and the needle in the center of the fine-tuning window, the string is in tune!

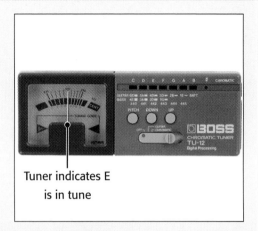

Tuner indicates E
is in tune

The chart that follows shows the tunings for the rest of the strings. If, for instance, the 5th string (also known as the A string) is flat, the indicator would point to A♭ or one of the other notes mentioned in the chart's Flat column. If the 5th string is sharp, the indicator would point to A♯ or one of the other notes mentioned in the chart's Sharp column. If the tuning for the 5th string is correct, the indicator will point to A, as shown in the chart's "In Tune" column.

String	In Tune	Flat	Sharp
5th/A string	A	F♯/G♭, G, G♯/A♭	A♯/B♭, B, C
4th/D string	D	B, C, C♯/D♭	D♯/E♭, E
3rd/G string	G	E, F, F♯/G♭	G♯/A♭, A
2nd/B string	B	G♯/A♭, A, A♯/B♭	C, C♯/D♭
Both E strings, 1 or 6	E	C♯/D♭, D, D♯/E♭	F, F♯/G♭

Again, once you've got the right note in the chromatic pitch indicator, then get the fine-tuning indicator right in the center. That's it!

Here's a general rule to follow regarding which way to turn your tuning keys:

- For the High E, B, and G strings:

    If the pitch is too flat, turn the tuner clockwise.

    If the pitch is too sharp, turn the tuner counterclockwise

- For the Low E, A, and D strings:

    If the pitch is too sharp, turn the tuner clockwise.

    If the pitch is too flat, turn the tuner counterclockwise

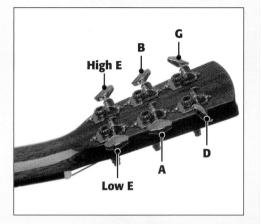

TIP

Make sure the tuner is close to the instrument. If you notice the pitch jumping around a lot, just stop the string and try again. Play the string at a normal volume, but don't hit it violently. The tuner's electronics need a healthy sound source for it to work properly.

This method of tuning uses comparing the string to be tuned with another string as a reference. This requires a bit more patience since you'll use your ear instead of the electronic tuner for guidance.

Tune to Another Instrument

Here's a way to tune your guitar without an electronic tuner, or when you're tuning to another instrument. Assume that your bottom E string is in tune with another guitar or piano. You'll get the rest of the strings in tune based on this string's pitch. First tune up the A string. Play the E string while putting a finger on the 5th fret.

This note is an A, so you'll try to tune the open A string to this pitch. Now play the open A string. If the open A string sounds higher than the E string, 5th fret, the A string is sharp. Lower the pitch by turning the A tuning peg clockwise until the two strings have the same pitch.

If the open A string sounds lower than the E string, 5th fret, the A string is flat. The A string needs to be tightened by turning the A tuning key until the strings have the same pitch.

Now continue the same process for the other strings. Tune the open D string to the A string, 5th fret.

Then tune the open G string to the D string, 5th fret.

The only exception occurs when you tune the B string. In this case, you'll tune the B string to the G string, 4th fret.

Finally tune the High E string to the B string, 5th fret.

CONTINUED ON NEXT PAGE

Step 1. Tune open A to E string, 5th fret.

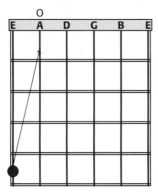

Step 2. Tune open D to A string, 5th fret.

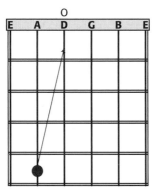

Step 3. Tune open G to D string, 5th fret.

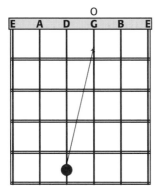

Step 4. Tune open B to G string, 4th fret.

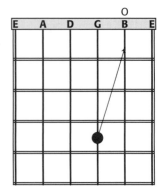

Step 5. Tune open High E to B string, 5th fret.

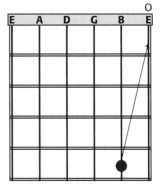

That's the whole process! This takes practice to hear the subtle difference in pitches, but can be done if you take your time and do it slowly.

Tuning an Electric Guitar

If you're tuning an electric guitar, you'll take a 1/4-inch cable and plug one end into the output jack of your guitar, then plug the other end in to the jack of the tuner. Make sure the volume control on your guitar is all the way up, and tune as if you were tuning your acoustic guitar.

TIP

If you notice your guitar is constantly going out of tune, or only certain chords will stay in tune, you need to change the strings. The strings have become fatigued and don't have the strength to stay in tune.

Getting Into Position

Before you start playing, take a moment to discuss proper positioning. A few key reminders will help you give your arms and hands more flexibility and reach.

Sitting Position

Because guitarists and guitars come in all different shapes and sizes, you need to do a bit of experimenting to figure out what works for you. Find a position that is easy on your hands, wrists, arms, and back.

Correct Sitting Position

When you start playing, you should be sitting in a comfortable position that allows you access to all parts of the guitar's neck without straining. Your back should be straight but relaxed. Your wrists should not be overly bent. Extreme angles in your wrists will impede the muscles in your hands.

For steel-string players, let the lower curve of the guitar rest against the leg under your picking hand (the right leg for right-handed guitarists, and vice versa).

The fretting hand of a steel-string guitarist should not have to support or lift up the neck. Its only job should be to press down on the strings. The guitar can be adequately cradled between the player's leg, chest, and the upper part of the arm.

CONTINUED ON NEXT PAGE

Classical guitarists usually elevate the foot below their fretting hand (the left foot for right-handed guitarists, and vice versa) on an adjustable footstool. You can now balance the guitar between your two thighs, and your fretting hand can move freely across the neck. Your picking hand is also able to float freely above the strings, as is necessary for classical technique.

Correct Viewing of the Neck

Many guitarists, as shown here, are tempted to crane their neck over their body to see what their fingers are doing over the guitar neck.

Others, as shown here, tilt the guitar in a more horizontal position, similar to a tabletop.

Try to avoid these positions because they inflict awkward angles on your neck, back, or wrists.

Your fingers will eventually learn where chords and notes fall on the neck, and you'll get used to the viewing angle of the neck. The correct viewing angle is shown here.

CONTINUED ON NEXT PAGE

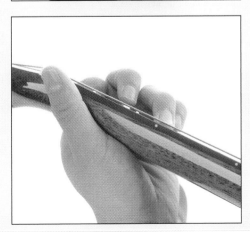

Sitting Position
(continued)

Before you pick up the guitar, try this "air guitar" test. Pretend you're playing guitar without the instrument and look at the angles in your wrists.

Once you're satisfied that both hands feel relatively comfortable, have someone place the guitar into your hands. To rest the guitar in the position you've picked, you may have to alter your sitting position by shifting your legs or angling the guitar.

Electric guitarists may need the help of a strap to achieve a proper sitting position, because the relatively small size of the electric guitar's body may make it sit lower in a person's lap.

Strap

TIP

Remember, since many electric guitars have smaller bodies than their acoustic counterparts, you may have less surface area to properly balance the guitar when you sit. This makes using a strap when you play even more important.

Standing Position

The same positioning principles of sitting apply to standing, except now you'll be using a guitar strap to achieve the best position. Use the strap to help put the guitar in the easiest place for your arms and hands to move around.

Use a Guitar Strap

Many guitarists, especially those who also sing, prefer to stand rather than sit. You can use a guitar strap to help balance the guitar around your neck and back. One end of the strap goes around the end pin of the guitar.

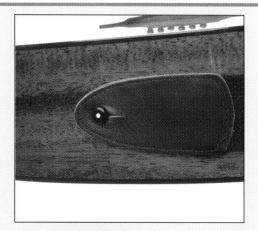

The other end of the strap can be tied around the neck by the tuning pegs (a), or hung around another pin where the neck meets the body (b).

Note: *Tying the strap around the neck may impede your fretting hand, especially when you're playing open chords. Adding a neck pin is usually a quick and inexpensive modification for an acoustic guitar. Electric guitars all come with two strap buttons. Most acoustics have only one.*

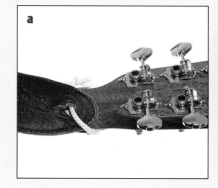

Hold the Guitar in Standing Position

As with the sitting position, make sure when you are standing that both of your hands can move comfortably across the instrument.

CONTINUED ON NEXT PAGE

Depending how long your arms are, you may want to slightly angle the guitar neck so you can easily access all parts of the fretboard.

Make sure the wrist of your fretting hand is not so low that you get a crooked wrist, which makes it hard to move your fingers. The photo gives you an example of a too low-slung neck.

CONTINUED ON NEXT PAGE

You can use the same "air guitar" test as described for the sitting position to hoist the guitar to its proper placement.

Air guitar test.

Proper standing pose with guitar.

Your fretting hand changes the pitch of the strings by placing pressure behind different frets. Here are some guidelines that will help you produce a clear tone with your fretting hand.

Fingers

Your fingertips should be placed directly behind any fret, without resting on top of the fret.

Your fingers should be gently curved, unless you're playing a barre—in which a finger is laid across more than one string (see Chapter 12 for more on barre chords). Use the fingertips, close to where the nail starts, but not the fingerpads.

CONTINUED ON NEXT PAGE

Thumb

The thumb's job lends support to the fingers' pressure on the fingerboard by pressing on the other side of the neck. For certain chords, the thumb may occasionally peek over the top of the neck. You probably won't be able to do this on a nylon-string guitar, which has a wider neck than an electric or steel-string guitar.

For playing barre chords (see Chapter 12 for more on barre chords), you'll want to keep your thumb behind the neck for extra support. For playing melodies, keeping your thumb in the back of the neck provides extra support and enables your fingers to stretch naturally along the length of the strings (see photo).

Note: *When your thumb is behind the neck, make sure that your wrist isn't bent severely when you change positions.*

If you hear a muffled tone on any string, there are several things you can check. Here are some clues and solutions to fretting finger-position problems.

1. Make sure you've put enough pressure on the string. If there's not enough, you'll hear a muted, percussive clunk.

2. Check that your finger is directly behind the fret. The farther the finger is from the fret, the more potential there is for the string in between to rattle. (a) shows improper placement; (b) shows proper placement.

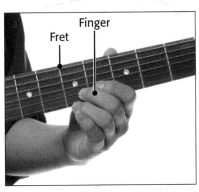

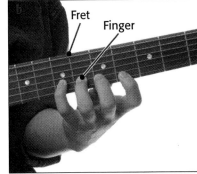

3. Make sure that other fingers aren't touching the string, as in (a). If you're playing with your fingertips, the other fingers will be arched over neighboring strings, as in (b).

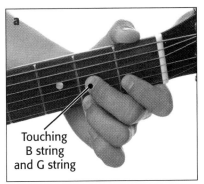

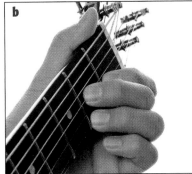

Picking Hand Position

Your picking hand has the job of producing the string's tone. Whether you use your fingers (finger-picking) or a pick, you'll want a stable reference point for your hand so it can develop consistent muscle memory of where to go to find a specific string without excess motion.

Fingerpicking Position

For fingerpicking, you have several options on how to position your hand. Classical guitarists let their hand float freely above the sound-hole, with their forearm braced against the upper bout of the guitar.

Other fingerpickers rest the heel of their palm on the bridge. Photo (a) shows how you should initially place the heel of your palm; (b) shows fingerpicking with the heel anchored.

Chapter 7 provides more information on fingerpicking.

Some fingerpickers brace their ring finger or pinky on the face of the guitar.

Use a Pick

If you use a pick, the best place to position your hand is on the bridge. By letting the heel of your palm rest on the bridge, your hand can quickly pivot to any string. Using a pinky or ring finger can hinder this freedom of movement with a pick.

Chapter 7 provides more information on how to use a pick.

chapter 5

Your First Chords

After you learn how to use a chord chart, you'll be able to show yourself how to find all the chords you need. I'll start off by showing you D, A7, and G, the easiest I, IV, and V chords to play in any key. You'll learn about I, IV, and V chords in a later chapter. For now, concentrate on learning how to read the chord chart and how to finger the three chords featured in this chapter.

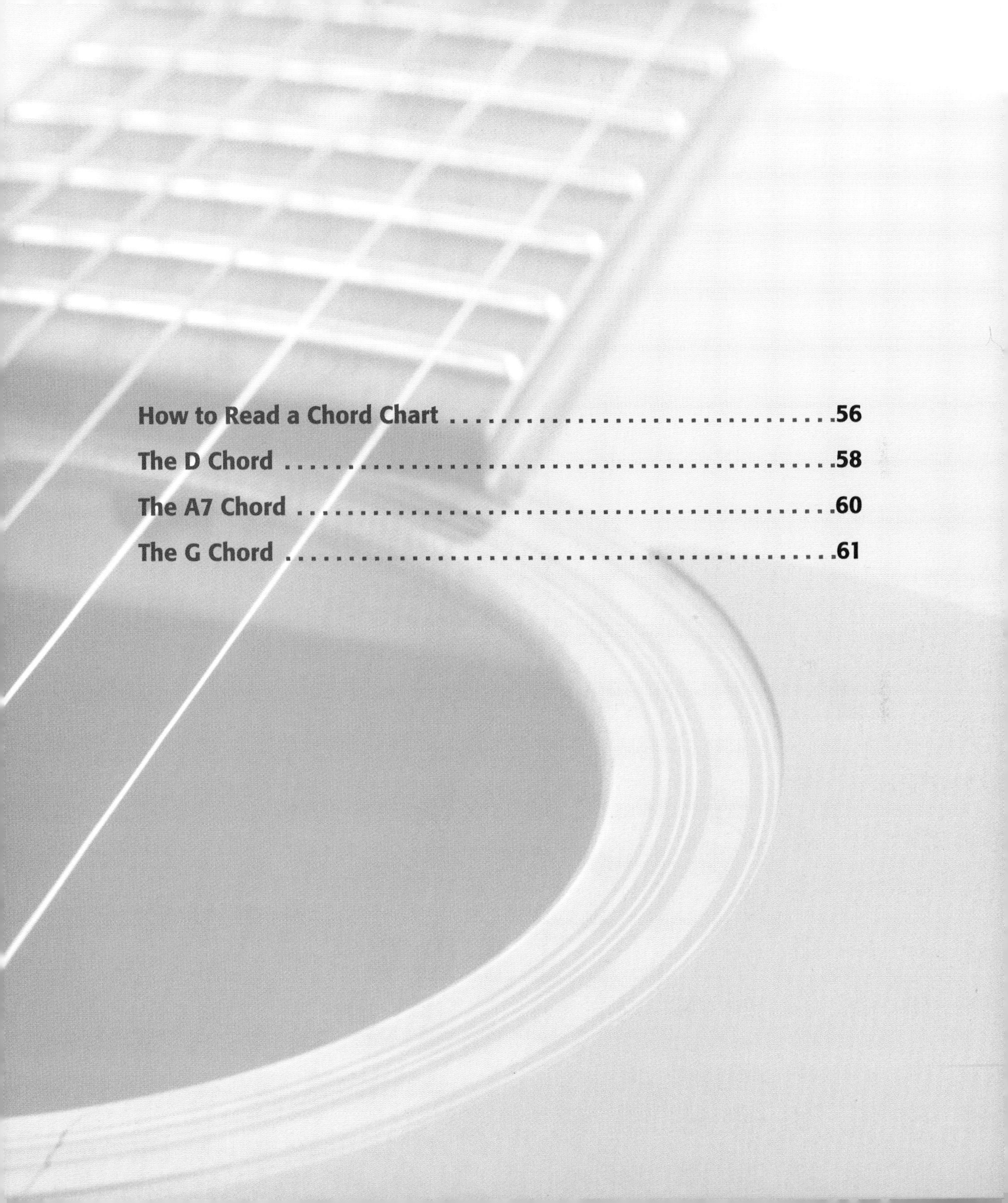

How to Read a Chord Chart

The chord chart represents the map of the fingerboard. It shows you which fingers to use, where to place them, and what strings to play. After you know the basics, you can use the chord chart to teach yourself any chord. That's all you need to know to use the chord chart to figure out any chord.

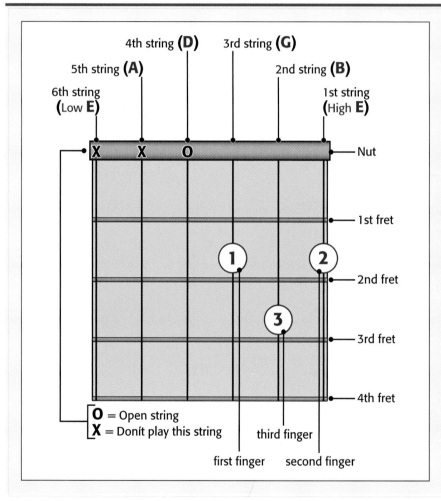

HIGH E STRING

The right line of the chart refers to the High E string, which we also call the 1st string. This is the string closest to your feet.

LOW E STRING

The left line refers to the Low E string, or the 6th string. This is the string closest to your face.

OTHER STRINGS

From left to right, each line represents your Low E, A, D, G, B, and High E string.

HORIZONTAL LINES

The top horizontal line represents the nut of your guitar. The other horizontal line directly underneath represents your 1st fret, and the lower lines represent the 2nd, 3rd, and 4th frets. This is the basic framework of the neck used for all chord charts.

X AND O

If you see an X above a particular string, you will not play that string. If you see an O above the string, it's an open string; that is, a string you will play, but you won't place a fretting hand finger on it.

DOTS AND NUMBERS

Any dots on the fretboard mean you should put a finger there, and the number above will tell you which fretting hand finger to use: 1 represents your index finger, 2 represents your middle finger, 3 represents your ring finger, and 4 represents your pinky.

TIP

Here are some tips for helping your hands learn a chord shape. (I'll show you how to do this on the following pages.)

1. One method is to put down your first finger, and then place the other fingers.

2. The other method is to place the finger that's on the string closest to the thumb (in this case it's the second finger). Then place the other fingers.

Depending on the chord, one method may help you place your fingers faster than the other.

The D Chord

Here is the chart for the D chord. First of all, notice the X's above the Low E (6th) and A (5th) strings. The presence of these X's means we won't strum or pick these strings at all. Next, notice the O above the D (4th) string. This means we can play this string without having to put a fretting hand finger on the string.

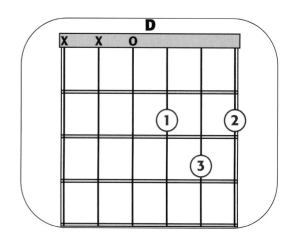

How to Finger the D Chord

Now we have to place three fingers to correspond with the three dots on the D chord chart. On the G string, there is a dot on the 2nd fret space. Because there is a 1 above it, place your index finger on that spot, right behind the 2nd fret.

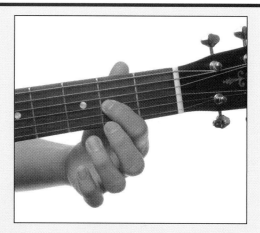

On the High E string, there is a dot on the 2nd fret. Because there is a 2 above that string, place your middle finger on that spot, right behind the 2nd fret.

Finally, on the B string, there is a dot on the 3rd fret. Because there is a 3 above that string, place your ring finger on that spot, right behind the 3rd fret.

There's your D chord! Now just play the bottom four strings. Remember, we're not playing the Low E and the A strings.

TIP

Remember to keep your fingers directly behind the appropriate fret for each string. This may be tricky when you start out, but just place them the best you can.

The A7 Chord

Now let's try the same with the A7 chord. This only needs two fingers to play. We won't be playing the Low E string (notice the X on the far-left string), and we don't need to place a finger on the A, G, and High E strings (notice the O's above the 5th, 3rd, and 1st strings).

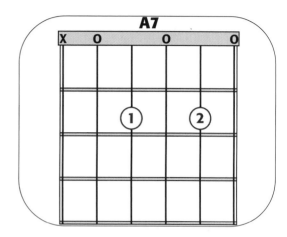

How to Finger the A7 Chord

On the D string, there is a dot on the 2nd fret of the 4th string. Because there is a 1 above that string, place your first finger on that spot, right behind the 2nd fret.

Finally, on the B string, there is a dot on the 2nd fret of the 2nd string. Because there is a 2 above that string, place your middle finger on that spot, right behind the 2nd fret.

There's A7! Just strum the bottom five strings. Remember, we're not playing the Low E (6th) string.

Now let's do the G chord together. Take a look at the chord chart and then try it before turning the page to see if you did it correctly.

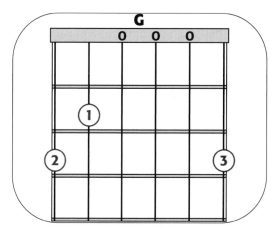

How to Finger the G Chord

The G chord uses all six strings, since there are no X's. The D, G, and B strings are played open (no fingers) because of the O symbols on top. First, on the A string, place your first finger on the 2nd fret of the 5th string.

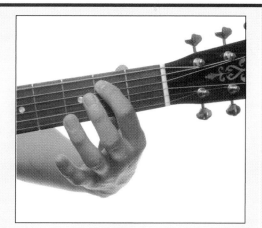

Then, on the Low E string, place your second finger on the 3rd fret of the 6th string (a).

Finally, place your ring finger on the 3rd fret of the 1st string (b).

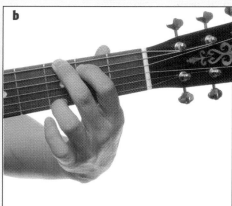

chapter

6

Moving Between Chords

Now that you've learned your first chords, let's look at the best way to move in between them. Whatever the chord combination, you'll want to find the most direct and efficient way of moving your fingers to and from each chord formation.

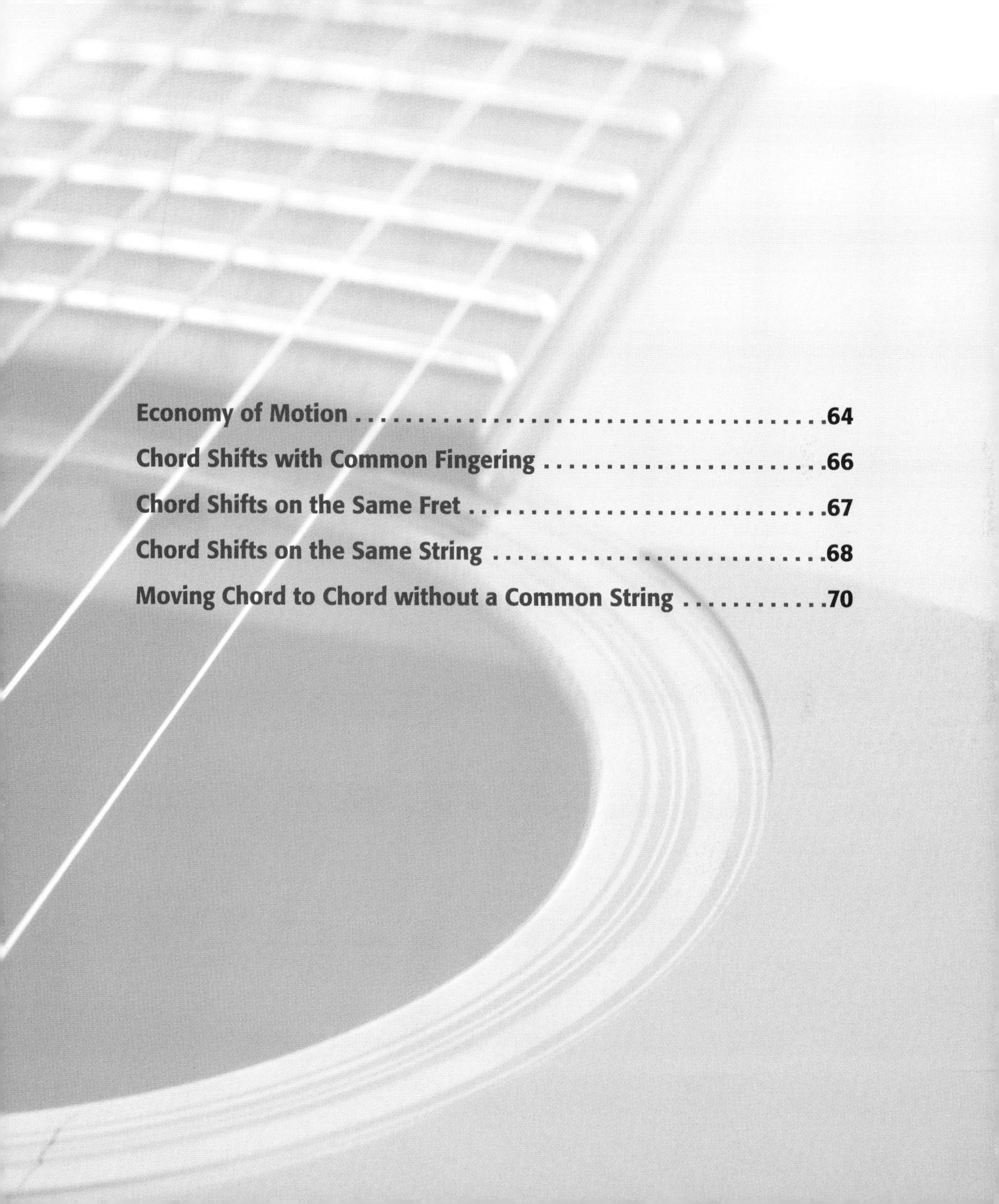

Economy of Motion

The more you move your fingers and hands, the more potential there is for error and delay. Do only the minimum lifting necessary to move your fingers in and out of different chord positions.

Relax Your Fingers

The less you have to move your fingers, the quicker you can transition between chords. When you lift your fingers, just raise them enough to clear the strings. You don't have to open the hand or pull the fingertip inches above the fingerboard. If you simply relax your hand, your fingers will lift up on the neck.

This photograph shows too much lifting of the hand when shifting chord positions.

Only a minimum amount of lifting is needed to change chord positions, as shown here.

To Move to an Adjacent String

If you are moving to an adjacent string on the same fret, just shift your finger up or down once you release the pressure of the finger. Photo (a) shows the first finger on the A string, 2nd fret. In (b), the first finger has shifted to the D string, 2nd fret.

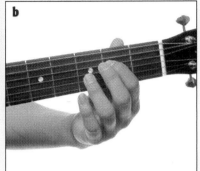

If you are moving to an adjacent fret on the same string, slide the finger up or down the string once you release the pressure of your finger.

Here you see the first finger on the G string, 2nd fret.

In this photo, the first finger has slid to the G string, 1st fret.

Some chord shifts are easy because some of the fingers don't move in between chords. The first three chords you learned all allow the first finger to stay on the 2nd fret. We'll start by shifting from the G chord, shown here.

Shift from G to Em

In this example the progression goes from G to Em (E minor; you'll learn this chord in Chapter 9). The G chord is shown above.

To play the Em chord, you won't need the second and third fingers to hold their positions in G, so relax those fingers, as shown in the photo. Remember, don't actively lift the fingers. This just adds one more task for your hand. Instead, relax your fingers, and they will naturally lift out of the way for you.

Now without lifting your first finger, place the second finger back on the D string, 2nd fret, and you have your Em chord. Remember that you're just pivoting on the first finger without lifting it.

Many beginner chord changes are easy because the fingers stay on a given fret. The first three chords you learned, D, A7, and G, all allow the first finger to stay on the 2nd fret. Shown here is the D chord.

Shift from D to A7

In this example, the progression goes from D to A7. The photo above shows the D chord fingering.

You won't need the third finger to play the A7, so relax that finger and let it lift up, as shown here. Remember, don't actively lift it. This just adds one more task for your hand. Instead, relax your finger, and it will naturally lift out of the way for you.

Move the remaining two fingers up one string each. Both fingers remain on the same fret. The first finger moves from the G (3rd) string to the D (4th) string, and the second finger moves from the E (1st) string to the B (2nd) string. Try moving the two fingers as a unit. Remember, just shift them upward to their new strings. You don't have to lift them up more than a few millimeters (a).

Now press down, and you're at the A7 chord (b)!

a

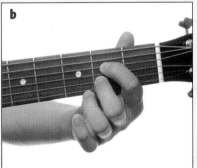

b

Chord Shifts on the Same String

Many beginner chord changes are easy because a finger stays on a given string on both chords. In these cases, you don't need to lift that particular finger.

Shift from D to E7

In some chord changes, a finger can remain on a string without lifting the finger. Try moving from D to E7 (you'll learn this chord in Chapter 9). Here is the D chord fingering.

From the D chord, relax your second and third fingers and allow them to lift slightly, as shown here.

The remaining finger should slide from the 2nd fret to the 1st fret of the G string. Remember, you don't have to lift this finger at all. Just let it slide on the surface of the string back one fret toward the nut.

Now add the second finger to the A string, 2nd fret. This is the shape for E7. On this chord, you should strum all six strings.

Moving Chord to Chord without a Common String

When moving from chord to chord, especially when you don't have a common fret or string, you'll find it helpful to try two ways of moving your fingers.

Move First Finger First

The first method involves using your first finger first. Many people are the most adept with their first finger because of its predominance in everyday use. Concentrate moving your first finger to its appropriate place in the destination chord, then place the other fingers.

For example, if you are playing A7 (a) to E7 (b), you would move the first finger from the 4th string, 2nd fret to the 3rd string, 1st fret. Then move the other finger, from the 2nd string, 2nd fret to the 5th string, 2nd fret.

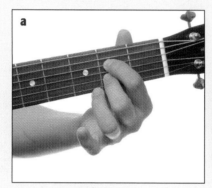

Move Furthest Finger First

The second method involves using your "furthest" finger first. This refers to the finger that wraps around the guitar the most, and is closest to your thumb. Since this finger has to do the most travelling across the neck, for many people it makes sense to move it before the others. Concentrate moving your farthest finger to its appropriate place in the destination chord, then place the other fingers.

For example, if you are playing A7 to E7, the second finger of the E7 is the furthest across the neck, so you would move that finger first.

You would move the second finger from the 2nd string, 2nd fret to the 5th string, 2nd fret. Then move the first finger from the 4th string, 2nd fret to the 3rd string, 1st fret.

Either of these methods may be easier for your fingers for any given chord combination. Whatever method works for you, work with your muscle tendencies instead of fighting them.

A Practice Strategy

If you're having trouble moving in between two particular chords, try adding fingers to the destination chord. For example, if you're having trouble between G and A (you'll learn this chord in Chapter 9), try alternating between the G chord (a) and just the first finger of A (b). Just strum all the same strings you would normally play for now.

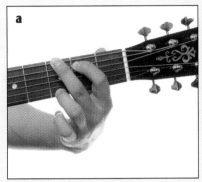

Once your fingers are used to that transition (a), go ahead and add the next finger as well (b).

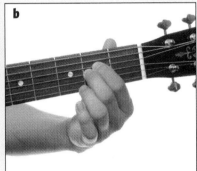

Once you can transition both of those fingers in the A chord smoothly (a), add the last finger to the A chord (b).

Using this method allows the individual fingers to learn their muscle memory gradually.

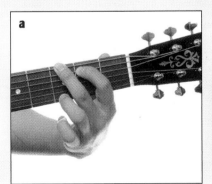

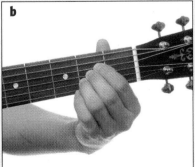

chapter 7

Strumming and Picking Technique

The hand that's not on the fretboard is in charge of the guitar's rhythm.
Whether you use your fingers or a pick, this hand has the job of making
your guitar groove and move in time.

Start Out with Your Thumb

Since you are still getting used to forming chords, you need to start with the most basic strumming hand technique. Here we use the pad of your thumb to strum chords, then we move on to using picks and fingerpicking.

G Chord Strum

Using the outer or higher edge of your thumb pad as you begin to play your chords produces a warm sound.

Start with the G chord, which uses all six strings.

1 Relax your arm and wrist. A tense arm or wrist results in a stiff sound.

2 Allow your thumb to hover above the 6th string.

3 Let the thumb drop from the 6th string all the way to the 1st string, allowing the thumb to give all six strings the same amount of vibration.

At the end of the strum, the thumb should be clear of the 1st string, but not too far away.

A CHORD STRUM 1

What if the chord doesn't use all six strings? Let's try an A chord (see Chapter 9), which uses the bottom five strings. Relax your arm and wrist again and allow your thumb to rest on the 5th string.

A CHORD STRUM 2

Let the thumb drop from the 5th string all the way to the 1st string, allowing the thumb to give all five strings the same amount of vibration. At the end of the strum, the thumb should be clear of the 1st string, but not too far away.

D CHORD STRUM 1

For a D chord, which uses the bottom four strings, relax your arm and wrist again and allow your thumb to rest on the 4th string.

D CHORD STRUM 2

Let the thumb drop from the 4th string all the way to the 1st string, allowing the thumb to give all four strings the same amount of vibration.

Play with a Pick

Playing with a pick helps you get a more focused sound and enables you to play faster rhythms. If you're a beginner, using a pick may feel strange at first, but you'll soon learn to strum and pick individual notes.

Most picks today are made with plastic or nylon and come in a variety of sizes and thicknesses.

Pick Strum

1. Hold the pick between the side of your first finger and the pad of your thumb. Grip about two thirds of the pick surface, allowing the tip of the pick to strike the strings.

2. Try not to tense your wrist and arm as you hold the pick. You won't be able to play dynamically and sensitively if your arm can't absorb the vibration from the strings. When you strum down (a) and up (b), your wrist should move more than your arm.

Anchor and Mute

ANCHOR

When you play individual strings for arpeggios (broken chords) or melodies, you may want to anchor your hand on the bridge; downstroke (a), upstroke (b). This will give you a consistent place to pick from, and your hand will get used to picking from one place and develop muscle memory.

MUTE

When you want to get a chunkier or drum-like sound, you can also use this position for a technique called muting. By slightly pressing down with the fleshy part of your palm on the string where it meets the bridge, you can create this more percussive, yet muted sound.

Fingerpicking

Fingerpicking allows the guitar's symphonic qualities to come out. By learning simple patterns, you can synchronize your thumb and fingers to play intricate patterns.

Fingerpicking Technique (Arpeggio)

Fingerpicking involves using the thumb and fingertips together. You've already started to use the thumb, so let's refine the technique. You use the junction of where your nail meets the skin to hit the string. The nail helps project the tone, while the skin gives the tone warmth.

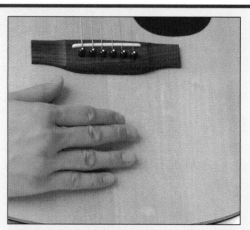

Try a G chord. Your thumb plays the 6th string, while your first and second fingers play the 3rd and 2nd strings, respectively.

First, let the thumb fall as it plucks the 6th string. You don't have to pull up on the string. Allow gravity to pull the thumb down.

Use the first finger to play the 3rd string. The finger should simply close in to the palm of the hand, without lifting the hand from the surface of the guitar. Notice the top of the hand doesn't rise.

Now, use the second finger to play the 2nd string. Again, the finger should simply close in to the palm of the hand. You've just played an arpeggio, a broken chord figure in which notes are played individually (one string at a time) instead of simultaneously. Repeat this pattern several times to create a cyclical, rhythmic effect.

chapter 8

Rhythm Guitar

Now that you know a few chords and how to strum the chords, let's put it together. Rhythm guitar is how you use various rhythms with the chords to accompany a melody in a song.

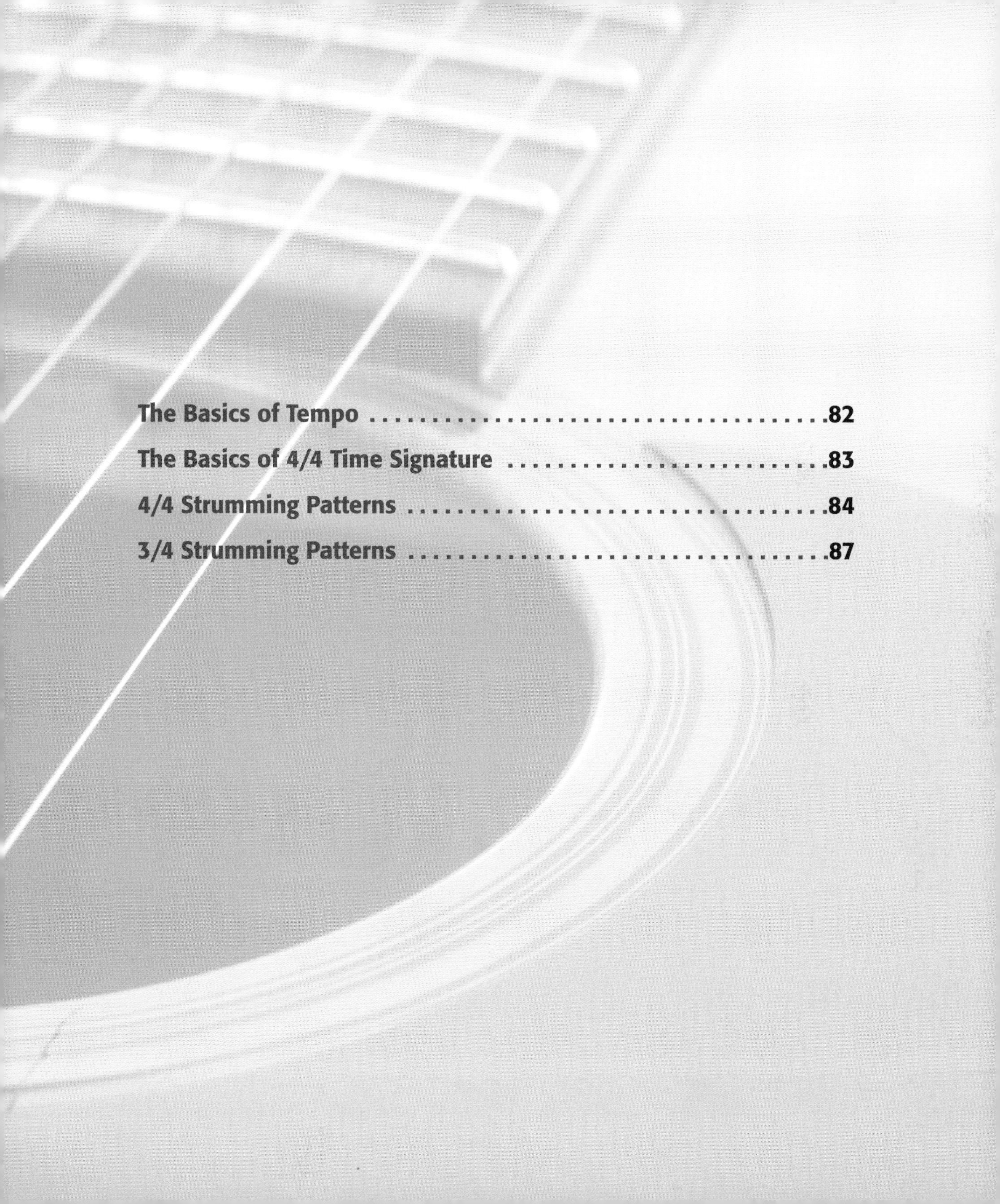

Playing in time and keeping a steady tempo can be tricky for the beginning guitarist. Here are some tips to keep in mind that will make playing rhythm guitar easier.

One of the basic challenges of playing rhythm guitar is keeping a steady tempo, the rate at which a song is played. This means not speeding up or slowing down within a given tune. As a tune progresses, most guitarists find that they want to speed up. This is a natural impulse when performing a repetitive function like strumming. Also, when guitarists reach the chorus of a song, they often react to the song's natural surge and play faster.

The best way to combat this natural tendency is to tap your foot in time during the song. Pretend that you're walking down the street. You usually don't vary your speed when you walk unless you make a conscious decision to do so. Since you've been walking longer than you've been playing guitar, your feet have very good muscle memory of keeping time.

Some people may feel awkward tapping their foot. Here are some alternate ways of keeping time:

- Tap your heel.
- Tap your toe inside of your shoe.
- Alternately tap your left and right feet, as if you were walking down the street.
- Rock side to side in your chair, as if you were dancing.

Now pretend you've got a piece of string tied between your tapping foot and your strumming hand. You can use this imaginary piece of string to synchronize the time in your foot to your strumming hand.

Most of today's popular music uses a 4/4 time signature. Here you learn where to emphasize and divide up your strumming to propel your rhythm guitar playing.

What 4/4 Time Is

In a 4/4 time signature, the rhythm is felt in groups of four beats per bar, the unit of rhythmic measurement:

Beats:	1	2	3	4	|1	2	3	4 etc.
	First Bar					Second Bar		

The first beat of every bar usually has the most rhythmic emphasis. (One notable exception is reggae, where the guitar and bass often do not play on the first beat.) The third beat is usually the second-most emphasized note.

Within every bar, there are four beats, which are synchronized with your foot taps. The halfway points of these beats are called "ands," and are represented by + symbols in the chart below. Notice that the +'s happen in between the down taps of the foot, when the foot comes back up:

Beats:	1	+	2	+	3	+	4	+
Foot:	Down	Up	Down	Up	Down	Up	Down	Up

When your foot goes down, you strum down.

When your foot lifts up, you strum up.

4/4 Strumming Patterns

Now let's take that information about 4/4 and start strumming. You use your foot tapping as a guide so you won't lose your sense of time.

Start by playing a simple strum on the first beat in each bar. Finger the G chord and strum when you see the V symbol. The V symbol indicates you should play a down stroke, where the pick goes from the sixth string all the way to the first string. Remember to keep time by tapping your foot and down strum when the first of four foot taps occurs. Repeat this pattern several times:

Beats:	1	+	2	+	3	+	4	+
Foot:	Down	Up	Down	Up	Down	Up	Down	Up
Strum:	V							

Once you feel you can play this in time, you can start subdividing the bar. The halfway point between the four beats is the third beat. Add a strum on the third beat, but let the first beat be the more prominent beat by using a bit more emphasis in that strum. Again, you're only strumming when the first and third foot taps occur. Repeat this pattern several times:

Beats:	1	+	2	+	3	+	4	+
Foot:	Down	Up	Down	Up	Down	Up	Down	Up
Strum:	V				V			

Keep going to get an even fuller rhythm pattern sound. Again, you subdivide the bar in the halfway point between the first and third beats. In other words, add the second and fourth beats, while keeping the first beat the most prominent. Now, every time the foot comes down, you're doing a down strum at the same time:

Beats:	1	+	2	+	3	+	4	+
Foot:	Down	Up	Down	Up	Down	Up	Down	Up
Strum:	V		V		V		V	

Now, for the first time, add the up strokes, indicated by the ^ symbols. Every time the foot comes down, you're doing a down strum at the same time, and every time the foot comes up, you're doing an up strum. When you play this set of alternating down strums and up strums, you are playing an eight-note pattern:

Beats:	1	+	2	+	3	+	4	+
Foot:	Down	Up	Down	Up	Down	Up	Down	Up
Strum:	V	^	V	^	V	^	V	^

To make this pattern sound more urgent, especially for rock rhythms, you can make all the strums down strums. You do a down strum when the foot comes down and a down strum when it comes up. This is a great rhythm in which to make a slightly percussive sound by slightly muting the strings where they meet the bridge:

Beats:	1	+	2	+	3	+	4	+
Foot:	Down	Up	Down	Up	Down	Up	Down	Up
Strum:	V	V	V	V	V	V	V	V

You can make other patterns that don't sound as busy or cluttered by removing some of the up strokes:

Beats:	1	+	2	+	3	+	4	+
Foot:	Down	Up	Down	Up	Down	Up	Down	Up
Strum:	V		V	^	V	^	V	^

Beats:		1	+	2	+	3	+	4	+
Foot:		Down	Up	Down	Up	Down	Up	Down	Up
Strum:		V	^	V		V	^	V	

CONTINUED ON NEXT PAGE

4/4 Strumming Patterns *(continued)*

Other patterns are less rhythmically obvious, or sound syncopated, if you remove some of the prominent downbeats, which is what is happening in the chart below: *Syncopation* occurs when the ear is drawn to a beat that is normally not emphasized. In other words, we can syncopate the rhythm by drawing attention to certain upbeats. In this example we eliminate the down strum on beat 3.

Beats:	1	+	2	+	3	+	4	+
Foot:	Down	Up	Down	Up	Down	Up	Down	Up
Strum:	V	^	V	^		^	V	^

In this example, we eliminate the down strum on beat 4.

Beats:	1	+	2	+	3	+	4	+
Foot:	Down	Up	Down	Up	Down	Up	Down	Up
Strum:	V	^	V	^	V	^		^

Here is another syncopated rhythm pattern to practice.

Beats:	1	+	2	+	3	+	4	+
Foot:		Down	Up	Down	Up	Down	Up	Down	Up
Strum:		V	^		^	V	^		^

TIP

One of the hardest things for many musicians is to keep a proper tempo. Most people tend to speed up during the course of a song (though some tend to slow down). Playing with a metronome, a device that produces a steady beat that you can play against, is a great way to develop the ability to play in time.

The second most common time sign is 3/4. As the name suggests there are only 3 beats per bar. This is commonly known as waltz time. Like 4/4, the first beat has the most emphasis.

The first example has a down strum on the first, second, and third beats.

Beats:	1	+	2	+	3	+
Foot:	Down	Up	Down	Up	Down	Up
Strum:	V		V		V	

The second example adds up strums on the "and" of the second and third beats.

Beats:	1	+	2	+	3	+
Foot:	Down	Up	Down	Up	Down	Up
Strum:	V		V	^	V	^

The last example adds up strums after each of the three beats.

Beats:	1	+	2	+	3	+
Foot:	Down	Up	Down	Up	Down	Up
Strum:	V	^	V	^	V	^

chapter 9

The Rest of the Open Chords

Here are the rest of the open chords, meaning those chords that have at least one open string. More chords are covered in Chapter 12, including barre chords.

Open chords, like the D, G, and A7 chords you first learned back in Chapter 5, all have an open string that's played.

A

First finger on 4th string, 2nd fret

Second finger on 3rd string, 2nd fret

Third finger on 2nd string, 2nd fret

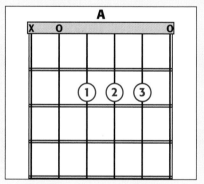

Play the bottom five strings (A-High E)

A7

First finger on 4th string, 2nd fret

Second finger on 2nd string, 2nd fret

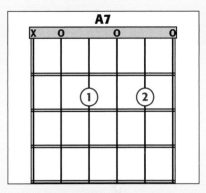

Play the bottom five strings (A-High E)

CONTINUED ON NEXT PAGE

TIP

While going through this chapter, you may wonder about some of the chord symbols you see. What is a G7 chord? What is an Am chord? What is AMaj7 and how is it different from A7? These questions will be answered in Chapter 10, "How to Read Chord Symbols, Tablature, and Lead Sheets."

AMaj7

First finger on 3rd string,
1st fret

Second finger on 4th string,
2nd fret

Third finger on 2nd string,
2nd fret

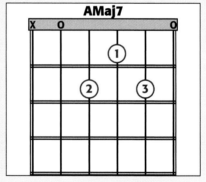

Play the bottom five strings
(A-High E)

Am

First finger on 2nd string,
1st fret

Second finger on 4th string,
2nd fret

Third finger on 3rd string,
2nd fret

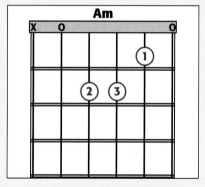

Play the bottom five strings
(A-High E)

CONTINUED ON NEXT PAGE

Am7

First finger on 2nd string,
1st fret

Second finger on 4th string,
2nd fret

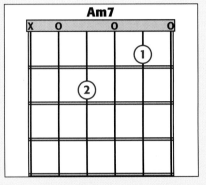

Play the bottom five strings
(A-High E)

B7

First finger on 4th string, 1st fret

Second finger on 5th string, 2nd fret

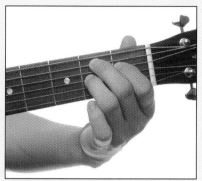

Third finger on 3rd string, 2nd fret

Fourth finger on 1st string, 2nd fret

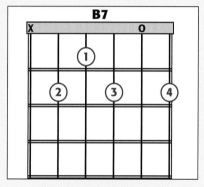

Play the bottom five strings (A-High E)

C

First finger on 2nd string,
1st fret

Second finger on 4th string,
2nd fret

Third finger on 5th string,
3rd fret

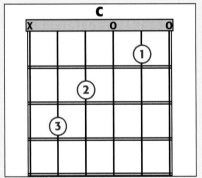

Play the bottom five strings
(A-High E)

C7

First finger on 2nd string, 1st fret

Second finger on 4th string, 2nd fret

Third finger on 5th string, 3rd fret

Fourth finger on 3rd string, 3rd fret

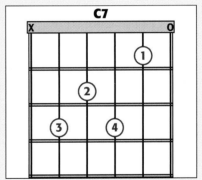

Play the bottom five strings (A-High E)

CONTINUED ON NEXT PAGE

CMaj7

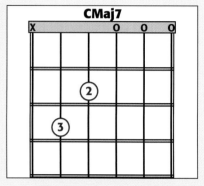

Second finger on 4th string,
2nd fret

Third finger on 5th string,
3rd fret

Play the bottom five strings
(A-High E)

D

First finger on 3rd string,
2nd fret

Second finger on 1st string,
2nd fret

Third finger on 2nd string,
3rd fret

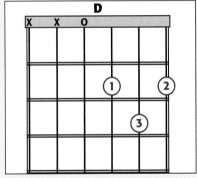

Play the bottom four strings
(D-High E)

CONTINUED ON NEXT PAGE

D7

First finger on 2nd string,
1st fret

Second finger on 3rd string,
2nd fret

Third finger on 1st string,
2nd fret

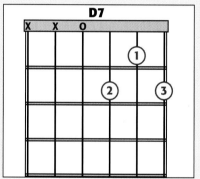

Play the bottom four strings
(D-High E)

DMaj7

First finger on 3rd string,
2nd fret

Second finger on 2nd string,
2nd fret

Third finger on 1st string,
2nd fret

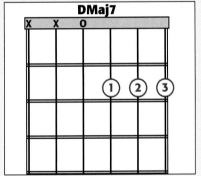

DMaj7

Play the bottom four strings
(D-High E)

CONTINUED ON NEXT PAGE

Dm

First finger on 1st string,
1st fret

Second finger on 3rd string,
2nd fret

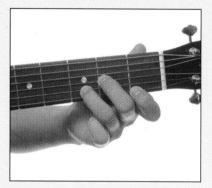

Third finger on 2nd string,
3rd fret

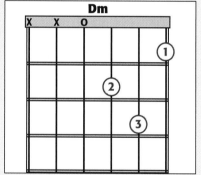

Play the bottom four strings
(D–High E)

E

*First finger on 3rd string,
1st fret*

*Second finger on 5th string,
2nd fret*

*Third finger on 4th string,
2nd fret*

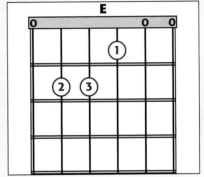

Play all strings

CONTINUED ON NEXT PAGE

E7

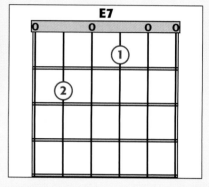

First finger on 3rd string,
1st fret

Second finger on 5th string,
2nd fret

Em

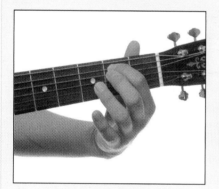

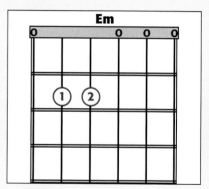

First finger on 5th string,
2nd fret

Second finger on 4th string,
2nd fret

Play the bottom five strings
(A-High E)

ALTERNATE Em

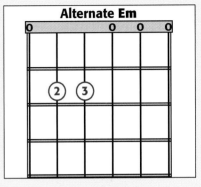

Second finger on 5th string,
2nd fret

Third finger on 4th string,
2nd fret

Play all strings

Em7

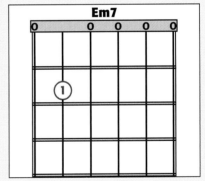

First finger on 5th string,
2nd fret

Play all strings

F

Technically F is not an open chord. As you can see by the chord chart, the first finger is covering two strings. The F chord is, however, usually taught before the other barre chords. You'll learn more about barre chords in Chapter 12.

First finger on 1st and 2nd strings,
1st fret

Second finger on 3rd string,
2nd fret

Third finger on 4th string,
3rd fret

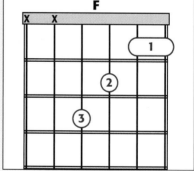

Play the bottom four strings
(D-High E)

FMaj7

First finger on 2nd string,
1st fret

Second finger on 3rd string,
2nd fret

Third finger on 4th string,
3rd fret

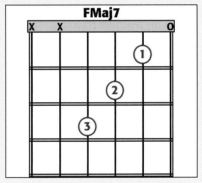

Play the bottom four strings
(D-High E)

G

First finger on 5th string, 2nd fret

Second finger on 6th string, 3rd fret

Third finger on 1st string, 3rd fret

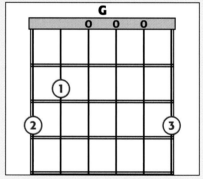

Play all strings

G7

*First finger on 1st string,
1st fret*

*Second finger on 5th string,
2nd fret*

*Third finger on 6th string,
3rd fret*

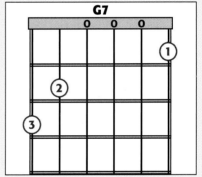

Play all strings

How to Read Chord Symbols, Tablature, and Lead Sheets

You've learned how to play some chords already. In this chapter you learn how to read chords and their symbols. You also learn how to read tablature, a graphic representation of how melodies are played on the fingerboard.

Five Common Types of Guitar Chords and Their Symbols

Chords have a specific language of symbols used to represent different sounds. Here's how to decipher the symbols for major, minor, dominant seventh, major seventh, and minor seventh chords.

Major Chords

Major chords are known for their generally bright, happy sound.

The 12 Major Chords
C
C♯ or D♭ (the same chord with two potential names)
D
D♯ or E♭ (the same chord with two potential names)
E
F
F♯ or G♭ (the same chord with two potential names)
G
G♯ or A♭ (the same chord with two potential names)
A
A♯ or B♭ (the same chord with two potential names)
B

Notice that the chord symbol doesn't need the word "Major" or "Maj" after it; that is, the major chord based on C is notated as "C," instead of "C Major" or "C Maj." The C, D, E, G, and A chords are all considered "open" major chords because there is at least one open string being played. All the other major chords are considered barre chords, in which your first finger is extended over more than one string. (Barre chords are discussed in Chapter 12.)

D

Minor Chords

Minor chords are known for their generally dark, sad sound.

The 12 Minor Chords
Cm
C#m or D♭m (the same chord with two potential names)
Dm
D#m or E♭m (the same chord with two potential names)
Em
Fm
F#m or G♭m (the same chord with two potential names)
Gm
G#m or A♭m (the same chord with two potential names)
Am
A#m or B♭m (the same chord with two potential names)
Bm

Notice that the chord symbol includes a lowercase "m" to signify it's a minor chord. The chord doesn't need the words "minor" or "min" after it; the symbol for the minor chord based on A is notated as "Am," not "A minor" or "A min." The Am, Dm, and Em chords are all considered "open" minor chords; all the other minor chords are considered barre chords (see Chapter 12).

Em

**CONTINUED
ON NEXT PAGE**

Dominant and Major Seventh Chords

Seventh chords are major chords with an extra note added. They are used for several different purposes, such as to help one chord want to resolve to another.

For example, play your G chord and then your C chord. Next, play G7 and then play C. The G7 version will want to go to the C because of its extra note.

Sometimes seventh chords are used because they have a funky, unstable sound. Pretend you have a progression that goes from A to D to E, then back to A. This is a relatively regular progression. Now make all of the chords into seventh chords: A7 to D7 to E7 back to A7. Your progression is much more bluesy with your chord modifications.

The dominant seventh chord has the same "happy" sound but sounds less resolved than a major chord, as if the chord was asking a question. Dominant seventh chords are commonplace in blues, jazz, and R & B chord progressions.

The other seventh chord is called a major seventh chord. This chord adds a wistful, sentimental, slightly sad feel to a major chord. You can start and end a song on this chord, but it will have a slightly melancholy, jazzy feel.

The 12 Dominant Seventh Chords	The 12 Major Seventh Chords
C7	CMaj7
C#7 or D♭7 (the same chord with two potential names)	C#Maj7 or D♭Maj7 (the same chord with two potential names)
D7	DMaj7
D#7 or E♭7 (the same chord with two potential names)	D#Maj7 or E♭Maj7 (the same chord with two potential names)
E7	EMaj7
F7	FMaj7
F#7 or G♭7 (the same chord with two potential names)	F#Maj7 or G♭Maj7 (the same chord with two potential names)
G7	GMaj7
G#7 or A♭7 (the same chord with two potential names)	G#Maj7 or A♭Maj7 (the same chord with two potential names)
A7	AMaj7
A#7 or B♭7 (the same chord with two potential names)	A#Maj7 or B♭Maj7 (the same chord with two potential names)
B7	BMaj7

Notice that the chord symbol includes the "7" to signify it's a seventh chord. The C7, D7, E7, G7, A7, and B7 chords are all considered dominant seventh chords as well as "open" seventh chords; all the other seventh chords are considered barre chords (see Chapter 12). A major seventh chord based on C has a symbol of CMaj7.

Minor Seventh Chords

Minor seventh chords are minor chords with an extra note added. They are usually not as dark or intense as a regular minor chord. They are often used in jazz, ballads, and more traditional popular music.

The 12 Minor Seventh Chords
Cm7
C♯m7 or D♭m7 (the same chord with two potential names)
Dm7
D♯m7 or E♭m7 (the same chord with two potential names)
Em7
Fm7
F♯m7 or G♭m7 (the same chord with two potential names)
Gm7
G♯m7 or A♭m7 (the same chord with two potential names)
Am7
A♯m7 or B♭m7 (the same chord with two potential names)
Bm7

Notice that the chord symbol includes the "m7" to signify it's a minor seventh chord. The Am7, Dm7, and Em7 chords are all considered "open" minor seventh chords; all the other minor seventh chords are considered barre chords (see Chapter 12).

A7

Am7

How to Read Tablature

Tablature is a notation system that shows the frets and strings on the guitar. It tells you where to place your fingers. Before you go very far in learning how to fingerpick or play melodies, it is useful to understand tablature.

What Tablature Shows You

Tablature tells you where to play notes on the fingerboard. It doesn't tell you how long to play each note and which finger to use.

Tablature uses six parallel lines. The top line represents the first string, and the lower lines represent the second, third, fourth, fifth, and sixth strings.

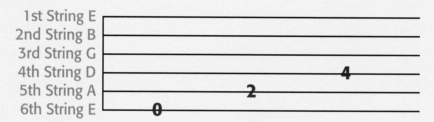

Events in tablature are read left to right.

1. In the previous example, the first thing that occurs is 0 on the low E string. The 0 indicates you play the open string; that is, a string with no frets depressed.

2. The next event is a 2 on the A string. This means you put a finger on the 2nd fret of the A string and then play the A string. You can use any finger, but for now use your first finger.

3. Finally, there is a 4 on the D string. This means you put a finger on the 4th fret of the D string and then play the D string. Use the third finger to play that fret, since it's an easy reach from the first finger on the A string.

Chords in Tablature

If you see numbers lined on top of each other, such as below, these are notes that should be played simultaneously.

```
1st String E ─────────────2───────────────
2nd String B ─────────────3───────────────
3rd String G ─────────────2───────────────
4th String D ─────────────0───────────────
5th String A ──────────────────────────────
6th String E ──────────────────────────────
```

For example, the notes above should all be played together in a single strum. These fingerings make up the formation of a D chord.

Below, the tablature shows that this chord is played as an arpeggio, since you play one note after another, not simultaneously.

```
1st String E ──────────────────────2──────
2nd String B ──────────────────3───────────
3rd String G ──────────────2───────────────
4th String D ─────────0─────────────────────
5th String A ──────────────────────────────
6th String E ──────────────────────────────
```

TIP

When you play a figure like the one above, where you're quickly crossing many strings, anchor the heel of your picking hand on the bridge so that your hand is stabilized.

How to Play a Song from a Lead Sheet

A lead sheet allows you to play a song by mapping out the chords of a song with the lyrics. This chapter illustrates how to read these charts.

Here's a lead sheet for the chart of "Sloop John B", a folk song that's also been made popular on the pop charts. Following this lead sheet there is an explanation of how to read it.

INTRO:

D	D		
We			

VERSE 1:

D	D	D	D
come on the sloop John	B, My	grandfather and	me, A-
D	**D**	**A7**	**A7**
round Nassau	town we did	roam.	Drinking all
D	**D**	**G**	**G**
night,	Got into a	fight.	Well I
D	**A7**	**D**	**D**
feel so broke up,	I want to go	home.	So

CHORUS:

D	D	D	D
hoist up the John B's	sail,	See how the mainsail	sets,
D	**D**	**A7**	**A7**
Call for the Captain a-	shore, Let me go	home,	let me go
D	**D**	**G**	**G**
home,	I wanna go	home, yeah	yeah, Well I
D	**A7**	**D**	**D**
feel so broke up	I wanna go	home.	

VERSE 2:

D	D	D	D
The first mate he got	drunk, And	broke in the Cap'n's	trunk, The
D	**D**	**A7**	**A7**
constable had to	come and take him a-	way.	Sheriff John

D	D	G	G
Stone,	Why don't you leave me a-	lone, yeah	yeah. Well I

D	A7	D	D
feel so broke up	I want to go	home.	So

CHORUS:

D	D	D	D
hoist up the John B's	sail,	See how the mainsail	sets,

D	D	A7	A7
Call for the Captain a-	shore, Let me go	home,	let me go

D	D	G	G
home, I wanna go		home, yeah	yeah, Well I

D	A7	D	D
feel so broke up	I wanna go	home.	The

VERSE 3:

D	D	D	D
poor cook he caught the	fits And	threw away all my grits ,	And

D	D	A7	A7
then he took and he	ate up all of my	corn.	Let me go

D	D	G	G
home,	Why don't they let me go	home?	This

D	A7	D	D
is the worst trip	I've ever been	on.	So

CHORUS:

D	D	D	D
hoist up the John B's	sail,	See how the mainsail	sets,

D	D	A7	A7
Call for the Captain a-	shore, Let me go	home,	let me go

D	D	G	G
home, I wanna go		home, yeah	yeah, Well I

D	A7	D	D
feel so broke up	I wanna go	home.	

CONTINUED ON NEXT PAGE

As with many pop songs, this tune is 4/4. Remember, this means chords are generally divided in groups of four, and the rhythmic emphasis is on the first beat.

Let's look at the introduction of the song, which has two bars of D, and the first four bars of the verse, also on D.

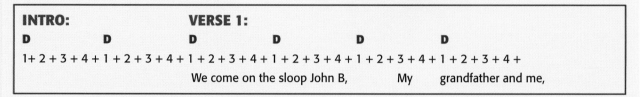

Don't worry too much about trying to synchronize your singing and playing when you first start out. You can use the word or syllable that lands on the first beat as a way to make sure your words are in time with the guitar. Remember, however, that sometimes, the sung melody doesn't start on the first beat. In this case, the word "we" actually starts before the first beat of the verse.

Start by playing a down stroke on the first beat of each bar.

```
INTRO:                    VERSE 1:
D           D             D           D           D           D
1+ 2 + 3 + 4 + 1 + 2 + 3 + 4 + 1 + 2 + 3 + 4 + 1 + 2 + 3 + 4 + 1 + 2 + 3 + 4 + 1 + 2 + 3 + 4 +
V           V             V           V           V           V
                          We come on the sloop John B,       My    grandfather and me,
```

Now add the third beat, but make sure the first beat is more prominent, by strumming slightly harder or by emphasizing the bass strings of the D chords (D and G strings).

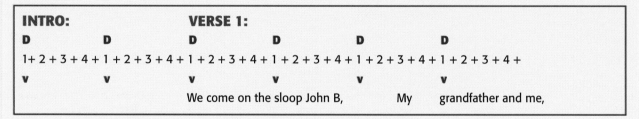

Now add the second and fourth beats.

INTRO: **VERSE 1:**

D	D	D	D	D	D
1 + 2 + 3 + 4 +	1 + 2 + 3 + 4 +	1 + 2 + 3 + 4 +	1 + 2 + 3 + 4 +	1 + 2 + 3 + 4 +	1 + 2 + 3 + 4 +
V	V	V	V	V	V
v v v	v v v	v v v	v v v	v v v	v v v
		We come on the sloop John B,		My	grandfather and me,

Try this pattern for the whole song. If it's hard to make a chord change, don't worry about strumming every beat, but keep time even when you don't strum the guitar. For example, look at the next phrase in the song:

D	D	A7	A7
round Nassau	town we did	roam	Drinking all
1 + 2 + 3 + 4 +	1 + 2 + 3 + 4 +	1 + 2 + 3 + 4 +	1 + 2 + 3 + 4
V	V	V	V
v v v	v v v	v v v	v v v

If you need more time to switch chords, don't slow down the tempo of the song by stalling after the fourth beat of the second bar. Instead, don't play the third and fourth beats of the second bar, and switch chords during that time.

D	D	A7	A7
round Nassau	town we did	roam	Drinking all
1 + 2 + 3 + 4 +	1 + 2 + 3 + 4 +	1 + 2 + 3 + 4 +	1 + 2 + 3 + 4
V	V	V	V
v v v	v switch	v v v	v v v

Remember, the song's time and tempo shouldn't stop for you. As your fretting hand gets faster, you can re-insert those strums.

CONTINUED ON NEXT PAGE

Often, you won't play four beats for every chord symbol. Here's one way it might be noted:

OUTRO:

D		**A7**		**|D**	**G**	**|D**
feel so broke up		I wanna go	home			

The bar lines around the D and G chords indicate that you'll divide the bar in half, so they each get two beats.

OUTRO:

D	**A7**	**‖D**	**G**	**|D**
feel so broke up	I wanna go home			

1 + 2 + 3 + 4 + 1 + 2 + 3 + 4 + 1 + 2 + 3 + 4 + 1 + 2 + 3 + 4

Other lead sheets may note irregular chord shifts by putting the chord directly over the word where the change occurs. Keep in mind your patterns should have

1. Primary emphasis on beat 1 (see underlining in the following patterns)

2. Secondary emphasis on beat 3

3. Less emphasis on the "and" of the beats

Try these different patterns. "D" stands for "downstroke," "u" stands for "upstroke."

1	+	2	+	3	+	4	+
D							

1	+	2	+	3	+	4	+
<u>D</u>				D			

1	+	2	+	3	+	4	+
<u>D</u>		D		D		D	

1	+	2	+	3	+	4	+
<u>D</u>	u	D	u	D	u	D	u

1	+	2	+	3	+	4	+
<u>D</u>		D	u	D	u	D	u

1	+	2	+	3	+	4	+
<u>D</u>		D	u	D		D	u

1	+	2	+	3	+	4	+
<u>D</u>		D	u	D		D	

1	+	2	+	3	+	4	+
<u>D</u>		D		D	u	D	

1	+	2	+	3	+	4	+
<u>D</u>		D	u			u	D

1	+	2	+	3	+	4	+
<u>D</u>		D	u	D		D	

More Fingerpicking

You learned some fingerpicking patterns back in Chapter 7. Now that you have learned how to read tablature, you can combine the two skills.

FINGERPICKING IN TABLATURE

Usually, you will want to play the root of the chord with your thumb. The root is the note with the same name of the chord. For example, the root of the Em chord is E, and the root of the D (major) chord is D. The following chart shows where the roots of different chords are found.

If the chord is:	Then the root should be played by the thumb on:
E, E7, Em	6th string
G, G7	6th string
A, A7, Am	5th string
B7	5th string
C, C7	5th string
D, D7	4th string

The pattern you learned at the end of Chapter 7 isn't the only pattern you can use for fingerpicking. You can call that first pattern T 1 2, since your order of picking was thumb, first finger, second finger.

Fingerpicking Patterns You Can Use

Here, you can apply a variety of finger-picking patterns to a popular song from the 1960s: "House of the Rising Sun," shown below. By using simple combinations of your thumb (T or 0), first finger (1), second finger (2), and third finger (3), you create both simple and complex patterns. The song is presented first; the finger picking patterns appear on subsequent pages.

Am   **Am**
There

VERSE 1:

Am	**C**	**D**	**F**
is a	house in	New Orleans	They
Am	**C**	**E7**	**E7**
call the	Rising	Sun,	and it's
Am	**C**	**D**	**F**
been the	ruin of	many a poor	boy, and
Am	**E7**	**Am**	**E7**
God, I	know I'm	one.	My

VERSE 2:

Am	**C**	**D**	**F**
mother	was a	tailor	She
Am	**C**	**E7**	**E7**
sewed my	new blue-	jeans.	My
Am	**C**	**D**	**F**
father	was a	gamblin' man	
Am	**E7**	**Am**	**E7**
Down in	New Or-	leans.	Now the

CONTINUED ON NEXT PAGE

VERSE 3:

Am	C	D	F
only	thing a	gambler needs	is a

Am	C	E7	E7
suitcase	and a	trunk.	And the

Am	C	D	F
only	time he's	satisfied.	Is

Am	E7	Am	E7
when he's	on a	drunk.	Oh

VERSE 4:

Am	C	D	F
mother	tell your	children	not to

Am	C	E7	E7
do what	I have	done.	

Am	C	D	F
Spend your	lives in	sin and miser-	y, in the

Am	E7	Am	E7
House of the	Rising	Sun.	There

VERSE 1:

Am	C	D	F
is a	house in	New Orleans	They

Am	C	E7	E7
call the	Rising	Sun,	and it's

Am	C	D	F
been the	ruin of	many a poor	boy, and

Am	E7	Am	
God, I	know I'm	one.	

Here is a thumb, first, and second fingerpicking pattern. The thumb plays either the 4th, 5th or 6th strings; the first finger plays the 3rd string, and the second finger plays the 2nd string.

T12

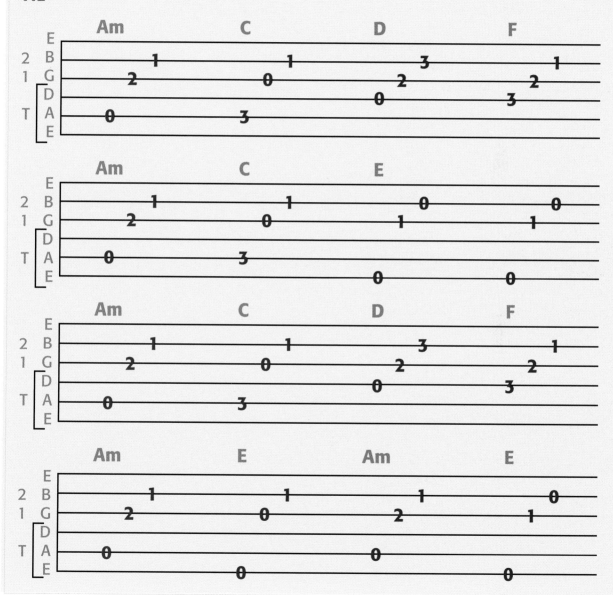

CONTINUED ON NEXT PAGE

Here is a thumb, first, second, and third fingerpicking pattern. The pattern is similar to the one you just did, but now the third finger will play the 1st string.

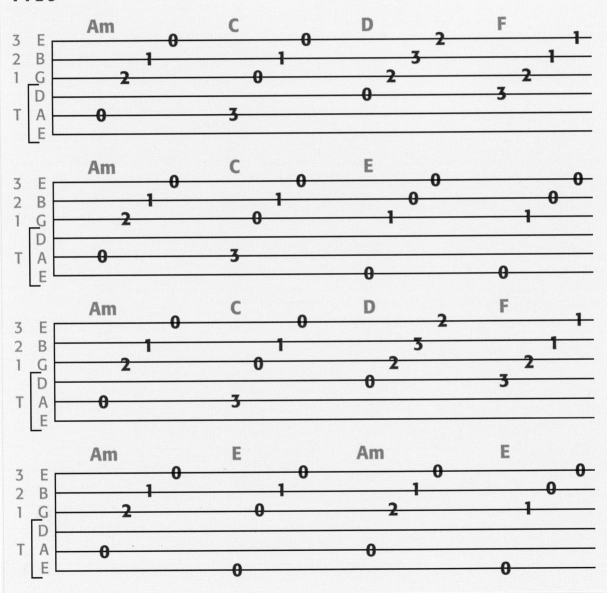

Finally, do thumb, first, second, third, second, and first.

T 1 2 3 2 1

chapter 11

Suspensions and Bass Runs

Now that you've learned your first chords, you can make them even more interesting. Suspensions create chordal tension and color, while bass runs connect and give chords momentum within a progression.

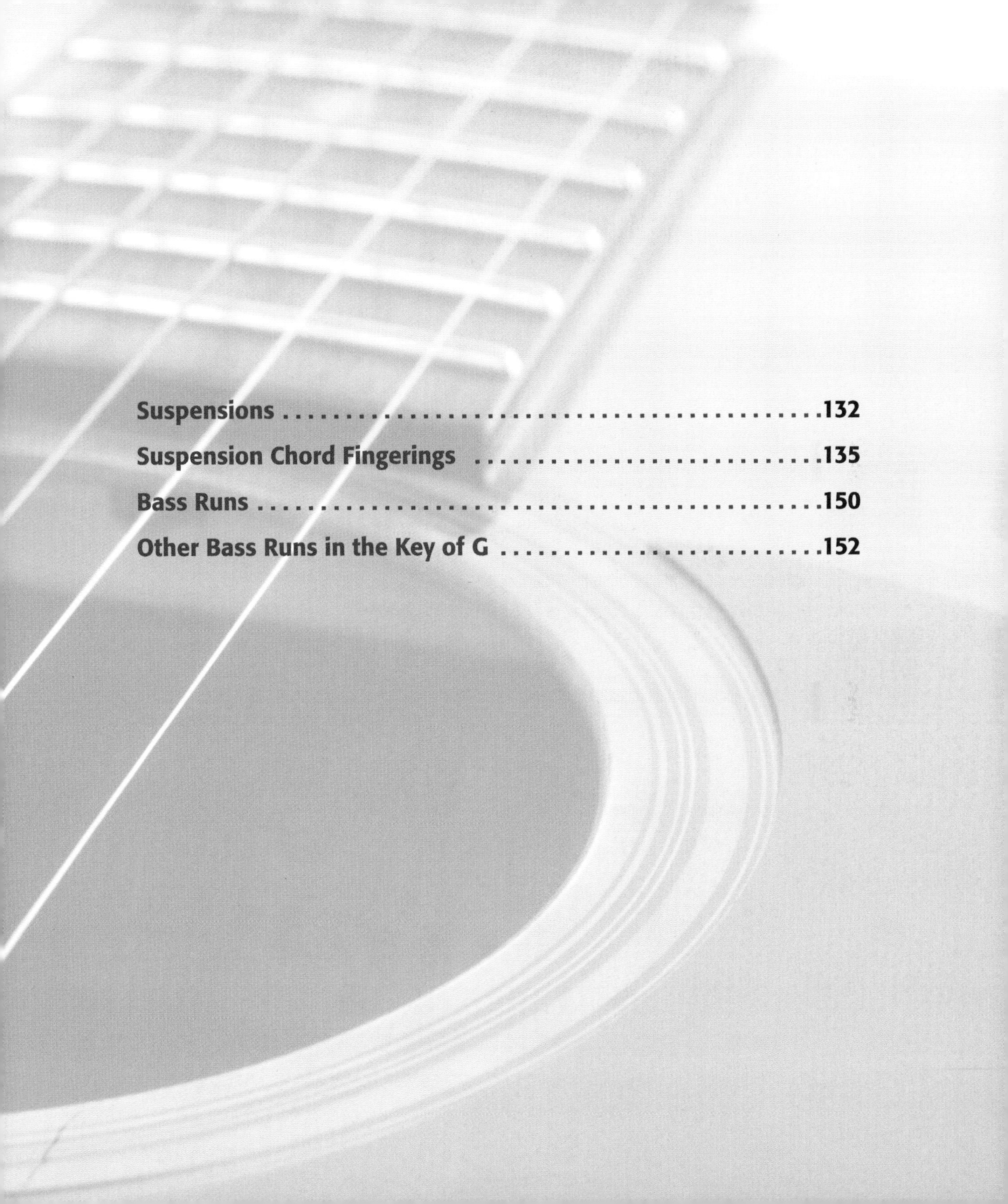

Suspensions

Suspensions add color to the chord or can sound like mini-melodies when they are used together. Many of the suspensions for your first chords can be made by either removing or adding another finger to the chord shape.

① Play your D chord, and you'll hear a chord sound that feels resolved. In other words, you can end a musical passage or song with this chord.

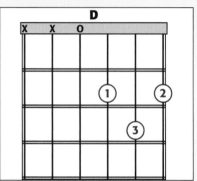

② Now play the D chord, but without the second finger on the 1st string, 2nd fret. This is called a Dsus2, a type of chord suspension. You may also see this chord described as Dadd2 or Dadd9.

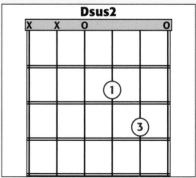

Notice that this chord seems to be floating up in the air. If you strum Dadd2 instead of D, you can make your chord seem more haunting or drifting. You can also use the Dadd2 chord in between strums of a regular D chord, as shown below. The slash marks stand for strums.

```
        D    D   Dsus2  D
        /    /    /     /
Beat    1    2    3     4
```

Now try another chord suspension. Go back to your original D chord and add your pinky to the first string, third fret. Now you have a suspension called Dsus4, which is commonly notated as Dsus.

This chord has an even floatier feel than Dadd2 and is out of tune for other chords. Again you can use this as a substitute for D, but it is more commonly used as a chord preceding or in between other D chords as shown below. The first shows 4 strums on

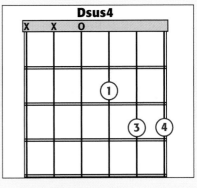

Dsus4

Dsus4, followed by 4 strums on D. The second shows 2 strums on D, 2 on Dsus4, 2 on Dsus2, and 2 on D. The double line signals the end.

```
        Dsus4                D
        /  /  /  /  |  /  /  /  /  |
Beat    1  2  3  4  |  1  2  3  4  |
        D      Dsus4  |  Dsus2  D      ‖
        /  /  /  /  |  /  /  /  /  ‖
Beat    1  2  3  4  |  1  2  3  4  ‖
```

Try placing suspensions anywhere you feel a chord needs more tension or harmonic contrast.

CONTINUED ON NEXT PAGE

Here's a general chart of the easiest suspensions to add to your beginning chords:

Chord	2	4
A, Am, A7, Am7	B	D
C, C7	D	F
D, D7, DMaj7, Dm	E	G
E, E7, Em, Em7	F♯	A
F	G	B♭
G	A	C

Note 1: *Whenever you add a sus2 to a seventh chord, you create a ninth chord.*

    Example 1: A7 + sus2 = A9

    Example 2: Em7 + sus2 = Em9

Note 2: *Usually a sus4 chord is notated as just "sus" (Dsus4 = Dsus), but I've kept the "4" in the chart to avoid confusion.*

Here are some common chords, followed by suspension chord fingerings.

A

First finger on 4th string, 2nd fret

Second finger on 3rd string, 2nd fret

Third finger on 2nd string, 2nd fret

Play the bottom five strings (A-High E)

Asus2

Remove third finger

Asus4

Add fourth finger to 2nd string, 3rd fret

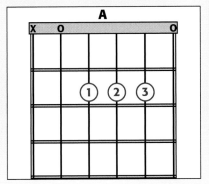

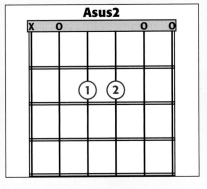

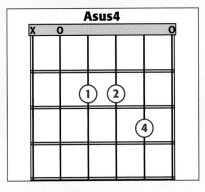

CONTINUED ON NEXT PAGE

A7

First finger on 4th string, 2nd fret

Second finger on 2nd string, 2nd fret

Play the bottom five strings (A-High E)

For an explanation of A9, see the chart on page 134.

A7sus2 (A9)

Remove second finger

A7sus4

Add third finger to 2nd string, 3rd fret

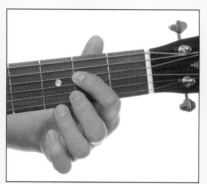

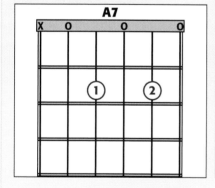

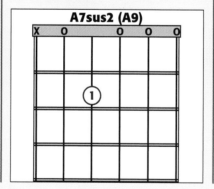

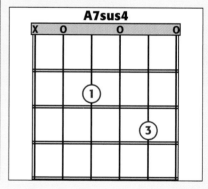

Am

First finger on 2nd string, 1st fret

Second finger on 4th string, 2nd fret

Third finger on 3rd string, 2nd fret

Play the bottom five strings (A-High E)

Amsus2

Remove first finger

Amsus4

Add fourth finger to 2nd string, 3rd fret

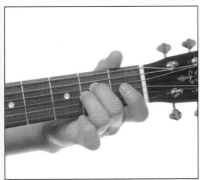

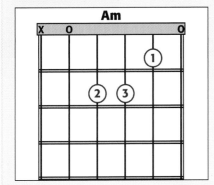

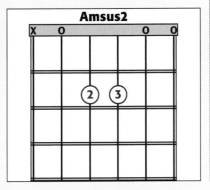

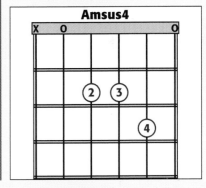

CONTINUED ON NEXT PAGE

Am7

First finger on 2nd string, 1st fret

Second finger on 4th string, 2nd fret

Play the bottom five strings (A-High E)

Am7sus2 (Am9)

Remove third finger

Am7sus4

Add third finger to 2nd string, 3rd fret

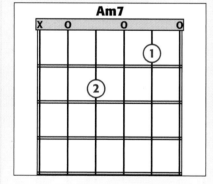

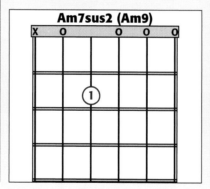

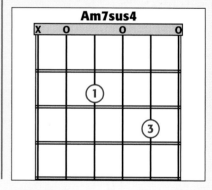

C

First finger on 2nd string, 1st fret

Second finger on 4th string, 2nd fret

Third finger on 5th string, 3rd fret

Play the bottom five strings (A-High E)

Csus2

Add fourth finger on B string, 3rd fret

Csus4

Add fourth finger on D string, 3rd fret

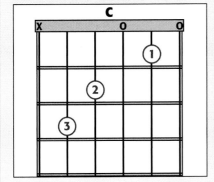

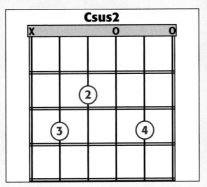

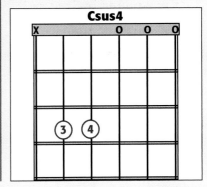

CONTINUED ON NEXT PAGE

D

First finger on 3rd string, 2nd fret

Second finger on 1st string, 2nd fret

Third finger on 2nd string, 3rd fret

Play the bottom four strings (D-High E)

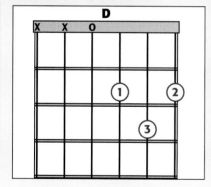

Dsus2

Remove second finger

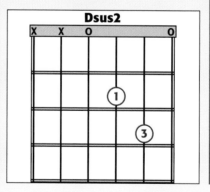

Dsus4

Add fourth finger on E string, 3rd fret

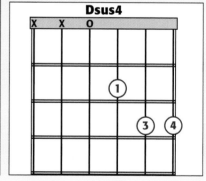

D7

First finger on 2nd string, 1st fret

Second finger on 3rd string, 2nd fret

Third finger on 1st string, 2nd fret

Play the bottom four strings (D-High E)

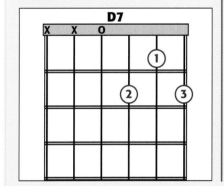

D7add2 (D9)

Remove third finger

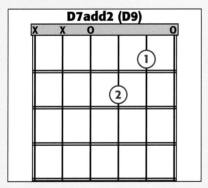

D7sus4

Add fourth finger on E string, 4th fret

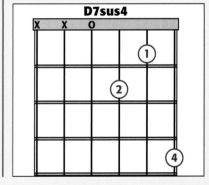

CONTINUED ON NEXT PAGE

DMaj7

First finger on 3rd string, 2nd fret

Second finger on 2nd string, 2nd fret

Third finger on 1st string, 2nd fret

Play the bottom four strings (D-High E)

For an explanation of DMaj9, see the chart on page 134.

DMaj9

Remove third finger

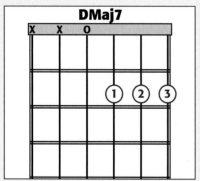

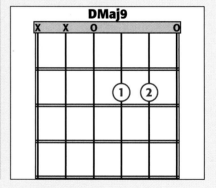

Dm

First finger on 1st string, 1st fret

Second finger on 3rd string, 2nd fret

Third finger on 2nd string, 3rd fret

Play the bottom four strings (D-High E)

Dmadd2

Remove first finger

Dmadd4

Add fourth finger on E string, 3rd fret

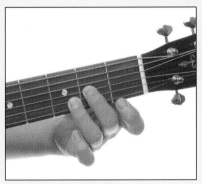

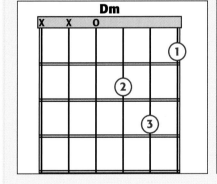

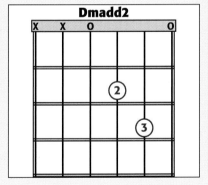

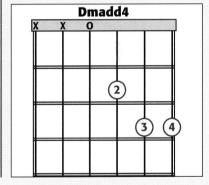

CONTINUED ON NEXT PAGE

E

First finger on 3rd string, 1st fret

Second finger on 5th string, 2nd fret

Third finger on 4th string, 2nd fret

Play all strings

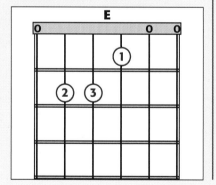

Esus2

Add fourth finger on 1st string, 2nd fret

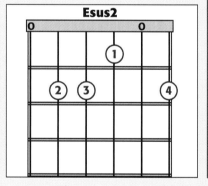

Esus4

Add fourth finger on 3rd string, 2nd fret

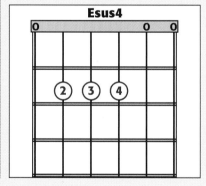

E7

First finger on 3rd string, 1st fret
Second finger on 5th string, 2nd fret
Play all strings

E7sus2 (E9)

Add fourth finger on 1st string, 2nd fret

E7sus4

Add third finger on 3rd string, 2nd fret

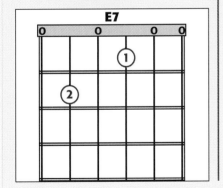

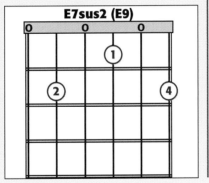

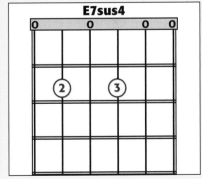

CONTINUED ON NEXT PAGE

Em

First finger on 5th string, 2nd fret
Second finger on 4th string, 2nd fret
Play all strings

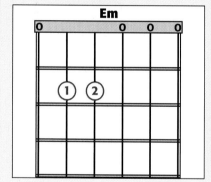

Emsus2

Add third finger on 1st string, 2nd fret

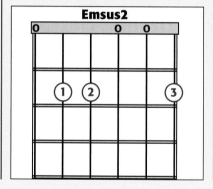

Emsus4

Add third finger on 3rd string, 2nd fret

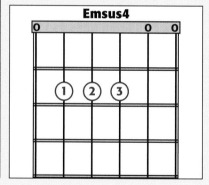

Em7
First finger on 5th string, 2nd fret

Play all strings

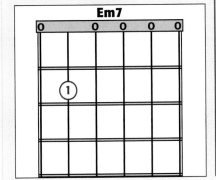

Em7sus2 (Em9)
Add second finger on 1st string, 2nd fret

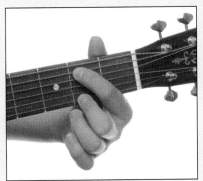

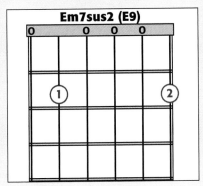

Em7sus4
Add second finger on 3rd string, 2nd fret

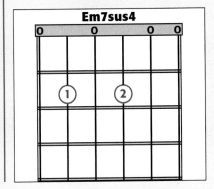

CONTINUED ON NEXT PAGE

F

First finger on 1st and 2nd strings, 1st fret

Second finger on 3rd string, 2nd fret

Third finger on 4th string, 3rd fret

Play the bottom four strings (D-High E)

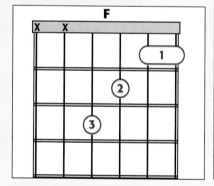

F

Fsus2

Add fourth finger to 1st string, 3rd fret, or remove second finger

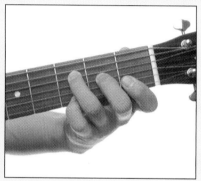

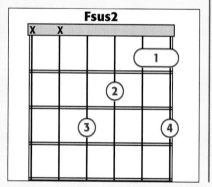

Fsus2

Fsus4

Add fourth finger to 3rd string, 3rd fret

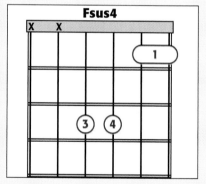

Fsus4

G

Second finger on 5th string, 2nd fret
Third finger on 6th string, 3rd fret
Fourth finger on 1st string, 3rd fret
Play all strings

Gsus4

Add first finger to 2nd string,
1st fret

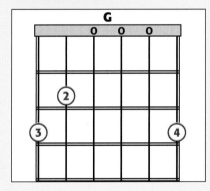

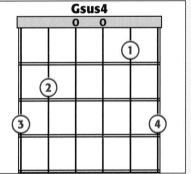

Bass Runs

Bass runs connect chords and help lead the ear along the chord progressions. Below are common bass runs in popular keys.

A bass run—a series of single notes played on the lower strings—is placed between two chords.

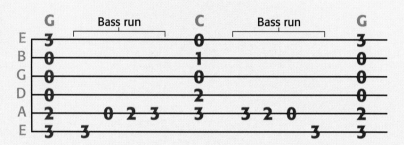

Here's an exercise you can do in the key of G, using the chords G and C.

1. First, strum the G chord.

2. Instead of immediately playing the C chord, you'll first play a three-note bass run. The first note of the bass run is the G note, on the 3rd fret of the 6th string.

3. The second note of the run is the A note played on the open 5th string.

4. The last note of the bass run is the B note on the 2nd fret of the 5th string.

5. Finally, play the C chord.

A great thing about this exercise is that you can play it forward and backward.

Other Bass Runs in the Key of G

Here are some bass runs in the key of G, using the common chords of G, C, D, and Em.

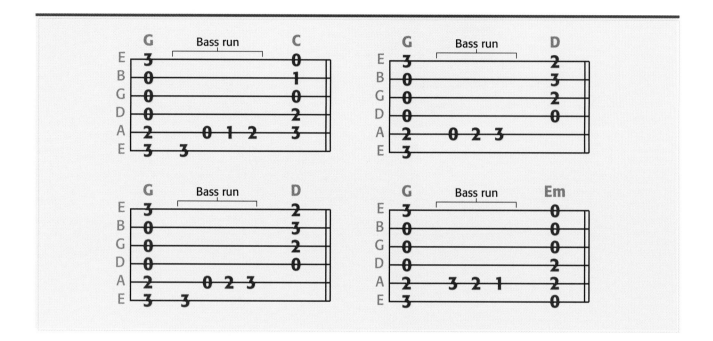

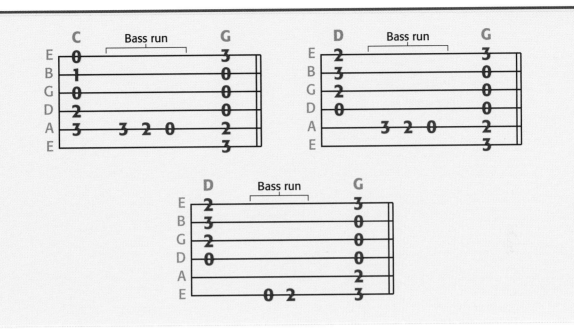

chapter 12

The Capo and Barre Chords

Not all chords can be played as open chords. This chapter will show you how to play them by using the barre chord technique. Barre chords allow you to take similar chord shapes and move them up and down the neck.

If you know only open chords, you may find that the chords do not match your vocal range when you try to sing as you play the guitar. The capo allows you to take the open chords you know and move them up and down the guitar neck.

What a Capo Is

A capo is a clamp that has a hard rubber surface that presses against the strings of a particular fret. It's held in place by a spring mechanism or an elastic band. The effect is that the capo becomes a moveable nut, shortening the scale of the guitar.

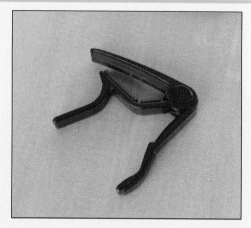

When you use your capo, place it right behind the appropriate fret, but not on the fret itself. Make sure you lift it cleanly over the strings before you fasten it to the neck, or it may throw off your tuning.

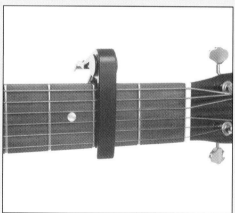

How a Capo Works

Here's how the theory of the capo works. The chords are moved up and down the *chromatic scale*. The chromatic scale is a musical scale in which pitches are divided into 12 equidistant steps. The notes of the chromatic scale are as follows:

C	C♯	D	D♯	E	F	F♯	G	G♯	A	A♯	B	C
	or		or			or		or		or		
	D♭		E♭			G♭		A♭		B♭		

When the capo is placed on the 1st fret, all your open guitar chords become one semi-tone higher. In other words, playing your C chord with a capo on the 1st fret becomes a C♯ or D♭ chord.

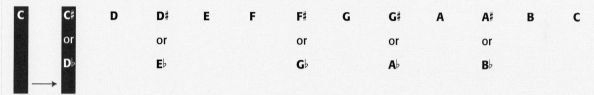

The distance between two adjacent notes is called a half-step (as above), which is the same as moving one fret.

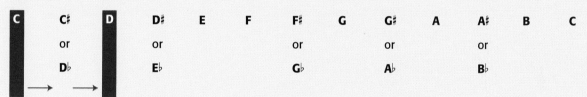

The distance between two half-steps is called a whole step (as above), which is the same as moving two frets.

CONTINUED ON NEXT PAGE

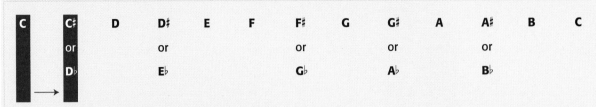

For every fret the capo is placed on, that's how far the chord is moved up the chromatic scale. For example, a C chord placed on the 1st fret moves up one step on the chromatic scale, which then becomes C♯ or D♭.

If you play the E chord on the 2nd fret, it moves up two half-steps on the chromatic scale and becomes F♯/G♭.

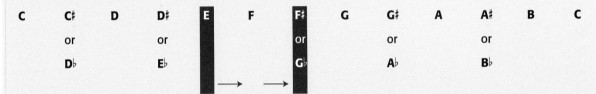

Let's say you're playing a song that uses the D, G, and A chords, but it's a little too low to sing against. Try moving it up three steps by placing your capo on the 3rd fret. You're still playing the D, G, and A shapes, but the actual chords all move up three half-steps each.

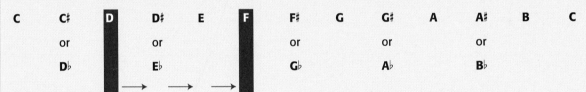

D moves up to F.

C	C♯	D	D♯	E	F	F♯	G	G♯	A	A♯	B	C
	or		or			or		or		or		
	D♭		E♭			G♭		A♭		B♭		

G moves up to A♯/B♭.

C	C♯	D	D♯	E	F	F♯	G	G♯	A	A♯	B	C
	or		or			or		or		or		
	D♭		E♭			G♭		A♭		B♭		

A moves up to C.

If the chords are still too low to sing against, continue moving the capo up. If the chords are too high to sing against, move the capo down. Most players don't place the capo higher than the seventh fret; if the chords are still too low to sing against, they'll choose to play the song in a different key.

The tables that follow illustrate what chords change to when using a capo.

A, Am, A7, OR Am7 CHORDS:

Capo on fret	A	Am	A7	Am7
1	A♯/B♭	A♯m/B♭m	A♯7/B♭7	A♯m7/B♭m7
2	B	Bm	B7	Bm7
3	C	Cm	C7	Cm7
4	C♯/D♭	C♯m/D♭m	C♯7/D♭7	C♯m7/D♭m7
5	D	Dm	D7	Dm7
6	D♯/E♭	D♯m/E♭m	D♯7/E♭7	D♯m7/E♭m7
7	E	Em	E7	Em7
8	F	Fm	F7	Fm7

B7 CHORD:

Capo on fret	B7
1	C7
2	C♯7/D♭7
3	D7
4	D♯/E♭
5	E7
6	F7
7	F♯/G♭
8	G7

CONTINUED ON NEXT PAGE

C OR C7 CHORD:

Capo on fret	C	C7
1	C♯/D♭	C♯7/D♭7
2	D	D7
3	D♯/E♭	D♯7/E♭7
4	E	E7
5	F	F7
6	F♯/G♭	F♯7/G♭7
7	G	G7
8	G7/A♭	G♯7/A♭7

E, E7, Em, OR Em7 CHORDS:

Capo on fret	E	Em	E7	Em7
1	F	Fm	F7	Fm7
2	F♯/G♭	F♯m/G♭m	F♯7/G♭7	F♯m7/G♭m7
3	G	Gm	G7	Gm7
4	G♯/A♭	G♯m/A♭m	G♯7/A♭7	G♯m7/A♭m7
5	A	Am	A7	Am7
6	A♯/B♭	A♯m/B♭m	A♯7/B♭7	A♯m7/B♭m7
7	B	Bm	B7	Bm7
8	C	Cm	C7	Cm7

G OR G7 CHORD:

Capo on fret	G	G7
1	G♯/A♭	G♯7/A♭7
2	A	A7
3	A♯/B♭	A♯7/B♭7
4	B	B7
5	C	C7
6	C♯/D♭	C♯7/D♭7
7	D	D7
8	D♯/E♭	D♯7/E♭7

Playing a barre chord involves using your first finger as if it was a moveable capo. These chords involve a slightly different finger and wrist technique than you use to play ordinary chords.

You will need to learn to play barre chords because there are some major and minor chords that can't be played as open chords and have to be played as a barre chord.

To Play a Barre Chord

Playing a barre chord involves laying the first finger across multiple strings. Let's concentrate on this technique before you play your first few barre chords.

1 Extend your first finger across the 2nd fret. This is called a 2nd fret barre. As with the other fingers, make sure the first finger is directly behind the 2nd fret, but not on top of it.

You may also wish to slightly roll your finger to the outside edge, which is closer to your thumb. This allows you to use the sharper edge of your finger, and apply more direct pressure than the broader surface under your finger.

CONTINUED ON NEXT PAGE

② Though it's all right to let your thumb peek over the top of the neck for open chords, you'll need to reposition your thumb for barre chords. The thumb should be directly behind the first finger, which means you drop the thumb lower behind the neck.

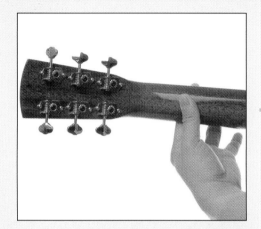

To accommodate this dropped-thumb position, you may also have to drop your wrist. If your wrist has a compressed or extreme angle, you may have to raise your arm position. All of these issues can easily be resolved if you're playing in a proper, upright position.

TIP

Because playing a barre requires an unusual muscle configuration that is not exercised in everyday use, the muscles needed to maintain a proper barre can take awhile to develop. Be patient. Here's a trick you can use while your hand gains strength: Use your forearm muscles to pull your first finger toward your chest.

F and Bm are often the first barre chords a beginner learns. In this chapter, each chord is shown in three stages that you can move between as your muscles get used to the barre techniques.

Don't feel as though you have to race to the full barre chord position. Take your time and move to the next level of chords only when you're ready.

F Barre Chord

BEGINNER F BARRE CHORD

One set of barre chords moves the E, Em, E7, and Em7 up and down the neck. You'll learn a beginner, interme- diate, and full barre chord for F, so your hands will have time to develop the requisite muscles. Here's the E chord you learned earlier (a) and the F chord as a barre chord (b). As you'll notice, the second, third, and fourth fingers are playing the shape previ- ously played by the first, second, and third fingers of the E chord. The extended first finger of the chord, known as the barre, essentially does the job of the nut in the E chord.

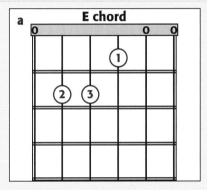

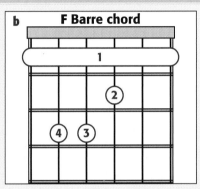

① Do the beginner F chord first. Put your first finger down on the B string, 1st fret.

CONTINUED ON NEXT PAGE

② Place your second finger down on the 3rd string, 2nd fret.

③ Now place your third finger on the 4th string, 3rd fret.

If you play the bottom four strings, you'll have a chord called FMaj7 (pronounced F major seventh). This is a great chord.

④ The final step is to play what's called a partial barre. Flatten your first finger so it covers the B and E strings at the 1st fret.

Remember, you'll probably need to drop your thumb and wrist so you'll be able to support that first finger.

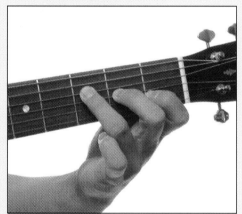

Apply pressure between your thumb and first finger. Now if you play the bottom four strings, you've got an F chord! This is the *beginner* F barre chord shape.

F BARRE CHORD SHAPE

Although you can use the beginner F chord now, let's continue looking at the other barre shapes.

1 From the beginner shape, move your third finger from the 3rd fret, 4th string to the 3rd fret, 5th string. Place your fourth finger on the 3rd fret, 4th string. Now you can play the lower five strings. This is the *intermediate* F barre chord shape.

2 To get the final shape, take the intermediate F chord shape and extend your first finger across all the strings. This is the *full* F barre chord shape.

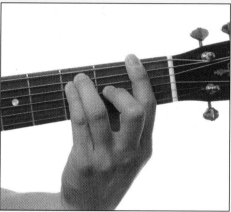

CONTINUED ON NEXT PAGE

If you go back to the F chord and lift up your fourth finger, you have the barre chord for F7 (pronounced F seven). Notice that it's just an E7 chord, using your first finger as a capo.

If you go back to the F chord and lift up your second finger, you have the barre chord for Fm (pronounced F minor). Notice that it's just an Em chord, using your first finger as a capo.

If you play only the bottom two (a) or three (b) strings, you have a modern chord hybrid, called the *power chord.* It's not technically a chord, because it's not a major or minor chord. The symbol for this chord is either F5 (pronounced F5) or Fno3 (pronounced F no three). I'll use the "5" designation. The power chord emerged in the late Sixties, when heavily distorted guitar tones came into vogue.

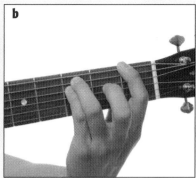

From this Fm shape lift up your fourth finger again, and you have the barre chord for Fm7 (pronounced F minor seven). Notice that it's just an Em7 chord, using your first finger as a capo.

CONTINUED ON NEXT PAGE

More E-Shape Chords

You can move these shapes you have just learned up and down the neck so your first finger is on the 2nd fret. You've taken your E shape, but moved its sound up two frets. You now have an F♯ chord (pronounced F sharp).

If you remove your fourth finger, you have an F♯7 chord (pronounced F sharp seven). If you remove your second finger, you have an F♯m chord (pronounced F sharp minor). If you play the bottom two or three strings, you have an F♯5 chord. If you remove your second and fourth fingers, you have an F♯m7chord (pronounced F sharp minor seven).

Full Barre F♯ chord

Full Barre F♯7 chord

Full Barre F♯m chord

F♯5 chord 2 strings

F♯5 chord 3 strings

F♯m7 chord

Here's the general chart for the E-shape barre chords:

First Finger	Barre on Fret	And then use one of these chords:			
	E	E7	Em	Em7	E5
1	F	F7	Fm	Fm7	F5
2	F♯/G♭	F♯7/G♭7	F♯m/G♭m	F♯m7/G♭m7	F♯5
3	G	G7	Gm	Gm7	G5
4	G♯/A♭	G♯7/A♭7	G♯m/A♭m	G♯m7/A♭m7	G♯5/A♭/5
5	A	A7	Am	Am7	A5
6	A♯/B♭	A♯7/B♭7	A♯m/B♭m	A♯m7/B♭m7	A♯5/B♭5
7	B	B7	Bm	Bm7	B5
8	C	C7	Cm	Cm7	C5
9	C♯/D♭	C♯7/D♭7	C♯m/D♭m7	C♯m7/D♭m7	C♯/D♭5
10	D	D7	Dm	Dm7	D5
11	D♯/E♭	D♯7/E♭7	D♯m/E♭m	D♯m7/E♭m7	D♯5/E♭5
12	E	E7	Em	Em7	E5

A-Shape Chords

BEGINNER Bm BARRE CHORD

The other set of barre chords moves the A, Am, A7, and Am7 shapes up and down the neck. Start this series of chords by learning the Bm chord. As with the E family of barre chords, take your time and move to the next level of chords only when you're ready.

1 Put your first finger down on the 1st string, 2nd fret.

CONTINUED ON NEXT PAGE

2 Next, place your second finger down on the 2nd string, 3rd fret.

3 Now place your third finger on the 3rd string, 4th fret. This is the *beginner* Bm barre chord shape.

If you play the three strings, you have a beginner Bm chord. Although you can start using the beginner Bm chord now, let's continue looking at the other shapes.

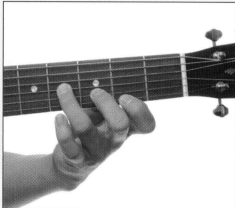

INTERMEDIATE AND FULL Bm BARRE CHORD
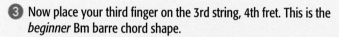

1 From the beginner shape, move your third finger from the 3rd string, 4th fret to the 4th string, 4th fret. Place your fourth finger on the 3rd string, 4th fret (where your third finger was). Now you can play the lower four strings. This is the *intermediate* Bm barre chord shape.

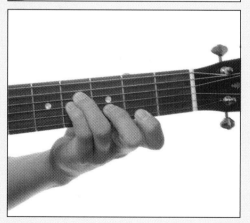

② To get the final shape, take the intermediate Bm chord shape, and extend your first finger across all the strings. This is the *full* Bm barre chord shape.

B, B7, Bm7 BARRE CHORDS

If you go back to the Bm chord shape; remove your second, third, and fourth fingers; and lay them down in the shape of an A chord; you have a B chord (a). You can also play the shape by laying down your third finger across the 2nd, 3rd, and 4th strings (b).

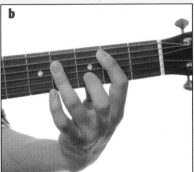

Go back to the Bm chord shape and remove your second, third, and fourth fingers again. Now place your third finger on the 4th string, 4th fret.

Now place your fourth finger on the 2nd string, 4th fret. You're placing an A7 shape above your finger and it's now a B7 chord.

CONTINUED ON NEXT PAGE

If you go back to the Bm chord and lift up your fourth finger, you have the barre chord for Bm7 (pronounced B minor seven). Notice that it's just an Am7 chord, using your first finger as a capo.

If you play only the bottom two (a) or three (b) strings, you have another set of power chords. The symbol for this chord is either B5 (pronounced B5) or Bno3 (pronounced B no three). We'll use the "5" designation.

TIP

The power chord can be used in two different settings:

1. If you find a major chord to be too "happy," but a minor chord to be too "sad," try using the power chord, which because of its composition is neither major or minor.

2. If you're playing distorted electric guitar and certain notes sound wobbly or seem to vibrate oddly, try the power chord. Because of the intermodulation of frequencies, distortion can make major and minor chords sound unstable. The power chord is less susceptible to this effect.

Here's the general chart for the A-based barre chords:

First Finger	Barre on Fret:	And then use one of these chords:			
	A	A7	Am	Am7	A5
1	A♯/B♭	A♯7/B♭7	A♯m/B♭m	A♯m7/B♭m7	A♯5/B♭5
2	B	B7	Bm	Bm7	B5
3	C	C7	Cm	Cm7	C5
4	C♯/D♭	C♯7/D♭7	C♯m/D♭m	C♯m7	C♯m7
5	D	D7	Dm	Dm7	D5
6	D♯/E♭	D♯7/E♭7	D♯m/E♭m	D♯m7/E♭m7	D♯5/E♭5
7	E	E7	Em	Em7	E5
8	F	F7	Fm	Fm7	F7
9	F♯/G♭	F♯7/G♭7	F♯m/G♭m	F♯m7/G♭m7	F♯5/G♭5
10	G	G7	Gm	Gm7	G5
11	G♯/A♭	G♯7/A♭7	G♯m/A♭m	G♯m7/A♭m7	G♯5/A♭/5
12	A	A7	Am	Am7	A5

chapter **13**

Chord Progressions

Chord progressions are used by guitarists to frame the melodies of songs. This chapter shows many commonly used chord progressions that you can use to decipher your favorite songs or to create your own songs.

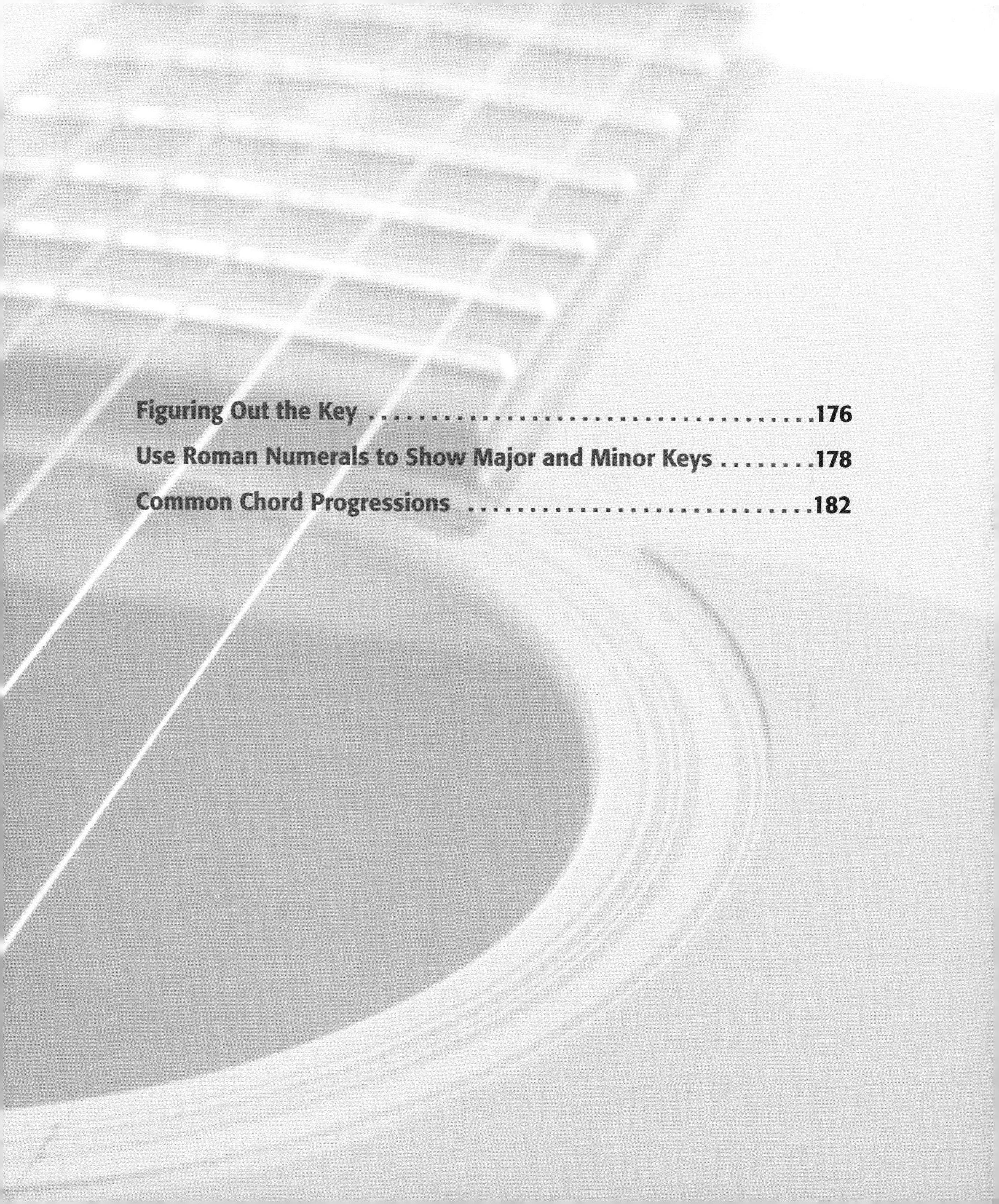

Figuring Out the Key

The key of a song helps you determine what chords are most likely to be used and what chord sounds the most resolved. The trick of figuring out which key your song is in is to determine what chord feels like "home." Listen to what chord makes the chord progression feel the most resolved or at rest. In many cases, the first or last chord in a section can provide a hint. However, this is not always true. In this chapter, you'll look at two examples, starting with "Sloop John B."

"Sloop John B"

INTRO:

D	D
We	

VERSE 1:

D	D	D	D
come on the sloop John	B, My	grandfather and	me, A-
D	**D**	**A7**	**A7**
round Nassau	town we did	roam.	Drinking all
D	**D**	**G**	**G**
night,	Got into a	fight.	Well I
D	**A7**	**D**	**D**
feel so broke up	I want to go	home.	So

CHORUS:

D	D	D	D
hoist up the John B's	sail,	See how the mainsail	sets,
D	**D**	**A7**	**A7**
Call for the Captain a-	shore, Let me go	home,	let me go
D	**D**	**G**	**G**
home,	I wanna go	home, yeah	yeah, Well I
D	**A7**	**D**	**D**
feel so broke up	I wanna go	home.	

"Sloop John B" uses the D chord as the first and last chord in both the verse and chorus. More important, the D chord sounds like the most resolved chord. Instead of ending on a D chord on the word "home" (the fifteenth chord in either the verse or chorus), try stopping the song prematurely on a G chord, like the one on bar 11 of the verse ("got into a fight"). You'll notice how the chord progression sounds like it's left dangling. It's not a bad sound, but it's not the way you're used to hearing conventional songs end.

Now try the same by stopping on an A7 chord, like the one on bar 14 (right after the phrase "I feel so broke up"). The A7 chord feels even more unresolved than the G chord. By process of elimination, you can start to hear how the D chord sounds like the home. Since the home chord is D, we are in the key of D Major.

Here are some of the most common major keys that you'll use as a beginning guitarist. This table will be explained in the following section:

Major key:	I	ii	iii	IV	V(7)	vi	vii°	♭VII	♭III	II(7)
C Major	C	Dm	Em	F	G(7)	Am	B°	B♭	E♭	D(7)
D Major	D	Em	F#m	G	Bm	Bm	C#°	C	F	E(7)
E Major	E	F#m	G#m	B(7)	C#m	C#m	D#°	D	G	F#(7)
F Major	F	Gm	Am	B♭	C(7)	Dm	E°	E♭	A♭	G(7)
G Major	G	Am	Bm	C	D(7)	Em	F#°	F	B♭	A(7)
A Major	A	Bm	C#m	D	F#m	F#m	G#°	G	C	B(7)

Using roman numerals is the traditional way of showing major and minor keys.

Let's examine just the key of D:

Major key:	I	ii	iii	IV	V(7)	vi	vii°	♭VII	♭III	II(7)
D Major	D	Em	F♯m	G	A(7)	Bm	C♯°	C	F	E(7)

Notice that in the key of D, you have the keys of D, G, and A7 for major chords. Using Roman numeral analysis, Roman numerals are placed above each of the chords. The D is called the I chord, "I" because it's the home chord; it's upper-case to signify that it's a major chord. The G is the IV chord and the A7 is the V7 chord. These are the primary major chords in the key of D.

There are also the minor chords Em, F♯m, and Bm. These are notated in lowercase Roman numerals to signify that they are minor. The seventh chord, C♯°, is called a *diminished chord,* which is not used much in modern popular music, although it's often used in jazz and pre-rock and roll popular music. A diminished chord sounds less resolved than a major or minor chord. Ending a song or a section of a song with a diminished chord is akin to ending a sentence with a question mark.

The last three chords are not always found in the key of D, but they are common exceptions in popular music. C and F, the ♭VII and ♭III chords (pronounced flat seven and flat three), are used in blues, hard rock, and other rock styles. The E (or E7) chord, the II chord in the key of D, is often used in pop music. The second chord in the key of D is usually a minor chord (Em), so the E or E7 gives an unexpected lift to a chord progression.

Analyze the "Sloop John B" progression now in terms of Roman numerals:

INTRO:

I		I	
We			

VERSE 1:

I	I	I	I
come on the sloop John	B, My	grandfather and	me, A-
I	I	V	V
round Nassau	town we did	roam.	Drinking all
I	I	IV	IV
night,	Got into a	fight.	Well I
I	V7	I	I
feel so broke up	I want to go	home.	So

Transpose to Major and Minor Keys

Transposition allows you to play a song in any key by moving the chords in the song. For example, in the key of A, the chords are:

Major key:	I	ii	iii	IV	V(7)	vi	vii°	♭VII	♭III	II(7)
A Major	A	Bm	C♯m	D	E(7)	F♯m	G♯°	G	C	B(7)

If you change the I, IV, and V chords to reflect the new key, you get this chord progression:

INTRO:

A   A

We

VERSE 1:

A	A		A		A	
come on the sloop John	B,	My	grandfather and	me,	A-	
A	A		E		E	
round Nassau	town we did		roam.		Drinking all	
A	A		D		D	
night,	Got into a		fight.		Well I	
A	E		A		A	
feel so broke up	I want to go		home.		So	

You have now transposed "Sloop John B" to the key of A.

The same thing can be done with minor keys, as you'll see next.

CONTINUED ON NEXT PAGE

"House of the Rising Sun"

INTRO:

Am   Am

       There

VERSE 1:

Am	C	D	F
is a	house in	New Orleans	They

Am	C	E7	E7
call the	Rising	Sun	and it's

Am	C	D	F
been the	ruin of	many a poor	boy, and

Am	E7	Am
God, I	know I'm	one.

This song is in the key of A minor. Every verse starts with Am, and the E7 at the end is used to set up the return of the next Am. Here are the most common minor keys:

Note: *The key is "A minor", but we still refer to the minor chord as "Am."*

Minor key	i	ii°	III	iv	v	VI	VII	V(7)
A minor	Am	B°	C	Dm	Em	F	G	E(7)
B minor	Bm	C#°	D	Em	F#m	G	A	F#(7)
C# minor	C#m	D#°	E	F#m	G#m	A	B	G#(7)
D minor	Dm	E°	F	Gm	Am	B♭	C	A(7)
E minor	Em	F#°	G	Am	Bm	C	D	B(7)
F# minor	F#m	G#°	A	Bm	C#m	D	E	C#(7)

This home chord is minor instead of major, so the Am chord is now notated as a lowercase "i."

INTRO:

i	i
There	

VERSE 1:

i	III	IV	VI	
is a	house in	New Orleans		They
i	**III**	**V**	**V**	
call the	Rising	Sun		and it's
i	**III**	**IV**	**VI**	
been the	ruin of	many a poor	boy,	and
i	**V**	**i**		
God I	know I'm	one		

You can play this song in any key, such as Em:

INTRO:

Em	Em
There	

VERSE 1:

Em	G	A	C
is a	house in New Orleans		They
Em	**G**	**B7**	**B7**
call the	Rising	Sun	and it's
Em	**G**	**A**	**C**
been the	ruin of	many a poor	boy, and
Em	**B7**	**Em**	
God I	know I'm	one	

CONTINUED ON NEXT PAGE

Common Chord Progressions

Here are some chord progressions used in different genres. You can use them as hints for figuring out other songs or as building blocks for creating your own songs.

FOLK

Here are some common chord progressions used in folk music.

I	I7	I	I
I	I	V	V
I	I7	IV	I
vi	IV	I	I ("Amazing Grace")
IV	I	V	I ("This Land Is Your Land")
I	I	IV	IV
V	V	I	I
I	I	V	V
V	V	I	I
I	I7	IV	IV
V	V	I	I
I	I	I	I
V7	V7	I	I
V7	V7	I	I

BLUES
Here are some twelve-bar blues patterns.

I	I	I	I7
IV	IV	I	I
V	IV	I	I

I	I	I	I7
IV	IV	I	I
V	IV	I	V

I	I	I	I7
IV	IV	I	VI7
II	IV	I	V

Minor:			
i.	VII	VI	V

ROCK
Here are some common chord progressions used in rock.

I	♭VII	IV	I

I	♭III	IV	I

Minor:			
i.	VII	VI	VI

An Introduction to Soloing and Improvisation

Now that you've learned to recognize keys and the chords within the key, you can start playing solos and learning to improvise. This section shows you how to apply the pentatonic scale to the right key, and how to create simple, effective melodies.

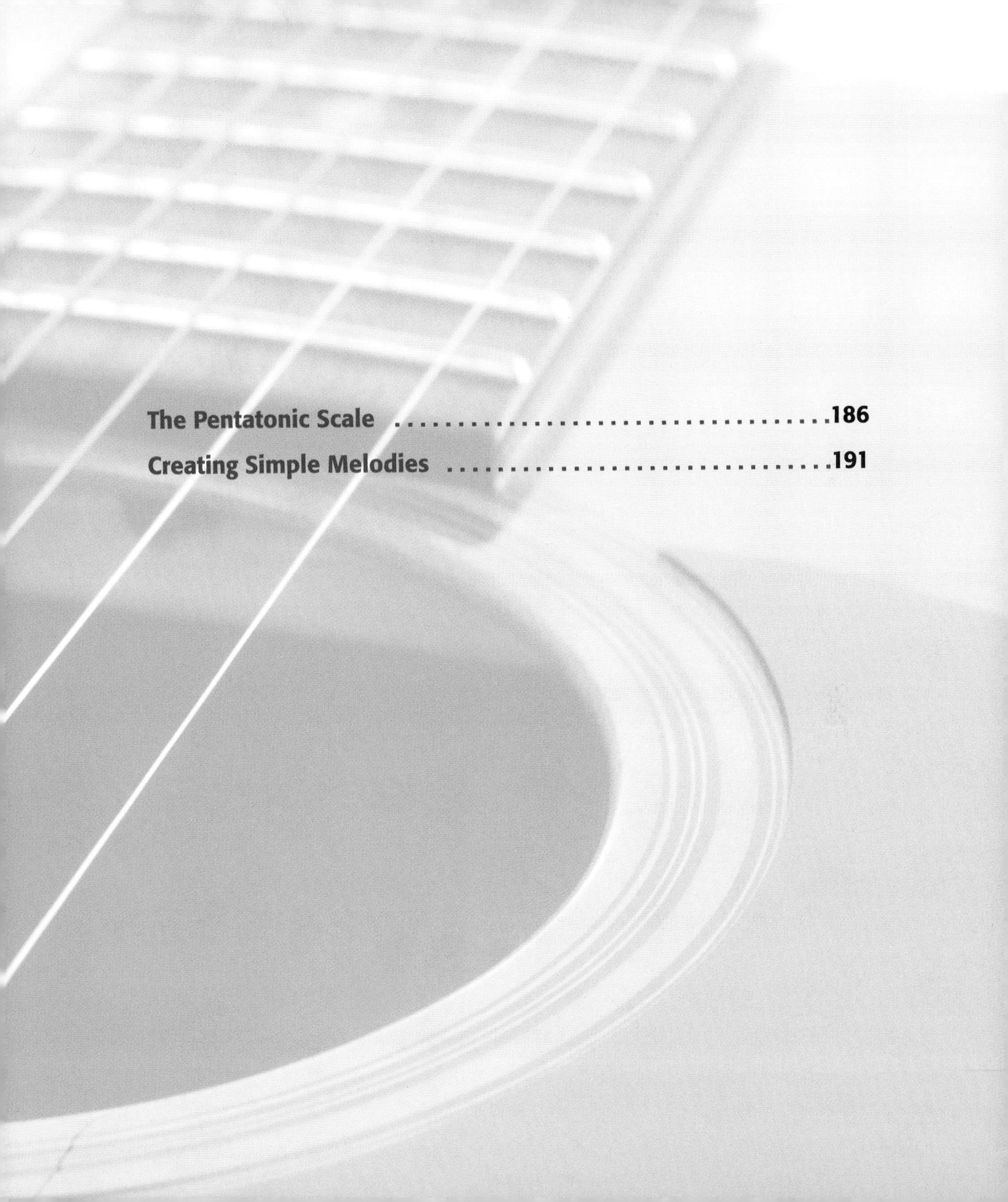

The Pentatonic Scale

The pentatonic scale is a simple five-note scale that has many applications across musical genres. In this section you learn to play it in moveable shapes across the guitar.

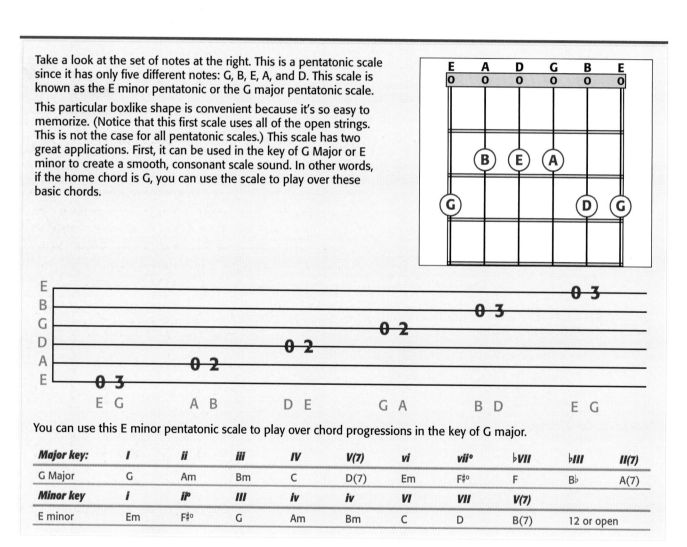

Take a look at the set of notes at the right. This is a pentatonic scale since it has only five different notes: G, B, E, A, and D. This scale is known as the E minor pentatonic or the G major pentatonic scale.

This particular boxlike shape is convenient because it's so easy to memorize. (Notice that this first scale uses all of the open strings. This is not the case for all pentatonic scales.) This scale has two great applications. First, it can be used in the key of G Major or E minor to create a smooth, consonant scale sound. In other words, if the home chord is G, you can use the scale to play over these basic chords.

You can use this E minor pentatonic scale to play over chord progressions in the key of G major.

Major key:	I	ii	iii	IV	V(7)	vi	vii°	♭VII	♭III	II(7)
G Major	G	Am	Bm	C	D(7)	Em	F#°	F	B♭	A(7)
Minor key	i	ii°	III	iv	iv	VI	VII	V(7)		
E minor	Em	F#°	G	Am	Bm	C	D	B(7)	12 or open	

Second, you can shift the scale shape up three frets to get a bluesier sound over the key of G. This scale is called the G minor pentatonic scale.

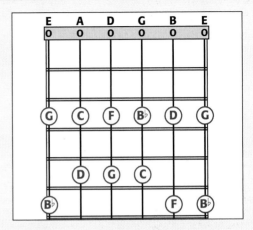

Now your notes are G, B♭, C, D, and F.

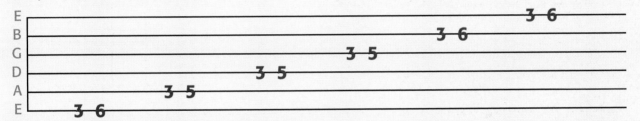

You can add one more note, called the "blue note," to create an even funkier, more dissonant sound. This scale is called the blues scale.

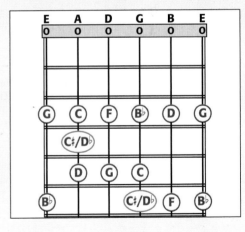

CONTINUED ON NEXT PAGE

The blues scale is called a moveable scale since it can be moved up or down depending on the key. Here is the G blues scale.

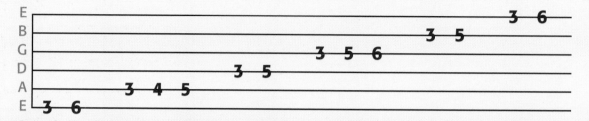

On the following page is a table that shows what chords and pentatonic scales can be used on each major key. For example, if you're in the key of C, the most likely chords are C, Dm, Em, F, G, and Am. You can also use B♭ and E♭ for blues or heavier rock, and also D or D7 for pop (the diminished chord of B° is rare in modern pop, so we won't use it here.)

There are three basic scale choices available in C. One is the major pentatonic scale, where your first finger is on the 5th fret, your third finger plays the 7th fret, and the fourth finger plays the 8th fret. This scale over these chords gives a melodic, consonant sound. You may hear musicians refer to this as sounding "in."

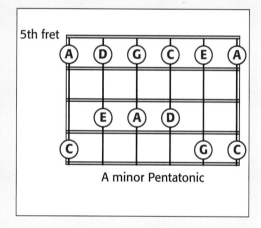

The second is the minor pentatonic scale, where your first finger is on the 8th fret, your third finger plays the 10th fret, and the 4th finger plays the 11th fret. This scale over these chords gives a darker, dissonant sound. You may hear musicians refer to this as sounding "out."

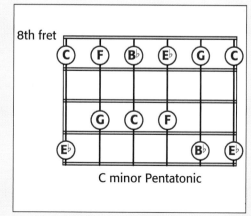

The third is the C blues scale, which looks like the minor pentatonic scale, with an extra note called the "blue note" of F♯/G♭ which makes the scale even darker and more dissonant.

Again, this table shows what chords and pentatonic scales can be used on each major key.

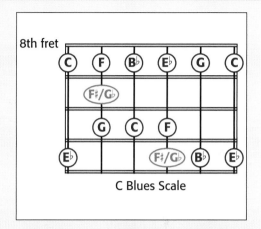

8th fret

C Blues Scale

Pentatonic scale starts on fret

Major key:	I	ii	iii	IV	V(7)	vi	vii°	♭VII	♭III	II(7)	Major	Blues
C Major	C	Dm	Em	F	G(7)	Am	B°	B♭	E♭	D(7)	5	8
D Major	D	Em	F♯m	G	A(7)	Bm	C♯°	C	F	E(7)	7	10
E Major	E	F♯m	G♯m	A	B(7)	C♯m	D♯°	D	G	F♯(7)	9	12 or open
F Major	F	Gm	Am	B♭	C(7)	Dm	E°	E♭	A♭	G(7)	10	1 or 13
G Major	G	Am	Bm	C	D(7)	Em	F♯°	F	B♭	A(7)	12 or open	3
A Major	A	Bm	C♯m	D	E(7)	F♯m	G♯°	G	C	B(7)	2	5

On the following page is a table that shows what chords and pentatonic scales can be used on each minor key. For example, if you're in the key of Am, the most likely chords are Am, C, Dm, Em, E7, F, and G. (The diminished chord of B° is rare in modern pop, so we won't use it here.)

There are two scales that are commonly used. The first is the minor pentatonic scale, where your first finger is on the 5th fret, your third finger plays the 7th fret, and the fourth finger plays the 8th fret. This scale over these chords gives a melodic, consonant sound on a minor chord. Notice that this is the same scale we used over the key of C Major. This is because the two keys are very closely related. In fact, they are referred to as relative major and minor scales.

CONTINUED ON NEXT PAGE

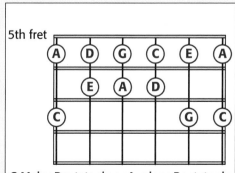

5th fret

C Major Pentatonic or A minor Pentatonic

The second is the A blues scale, which looks like the minor pentatonic scale, with an extra note called the "blue note" of D♯/E♭, which makes the scale even darker and more dissonant.

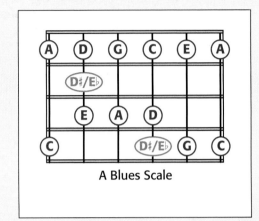

A Blues Scale

Pentatonic scale starts on fret

Minor key	i	ii°	III	iv	v	VI	VII	V(7)	For both minor and blues
A minor	Am	B°	C	Dm	Em	F	G	E(7)	5
B minor	Bm	C♯°	D	Em	F♯m	G	A	F♯(7)	7
C♯ minor	C♯m	D♯°	E	F♯m	G♯m	A	B	G♯(7)	8
D minor	Dm	E°	F	Gm	Am	B♭	C	A(7)	10
E minor	Em	F♯°	G	Am	Bm	C	D	B(7)	12 or open
F♯ minor	F♯m	G♯°	A	Bm	C♯m	D	E	C♯(7)	2

Creating Simple Melodies

Now that you know the vocabulary of the pentatonic scale, you can construct melodic phrases using motifs. A *motif* is a simple, memorable phrase that can be repeated, varied, or recombined to create larger melodic statements.

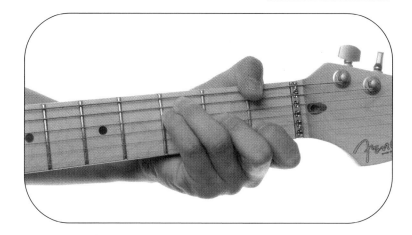

Create Your First Melody

Use your first scale of E, G, A, B, and D to create your first melody in E minor pentatonic.

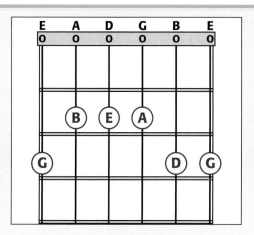

Let's say you compose a small motif phrase out of the previous set of notes, such as the one pictured here.

Original motif

```
E |---------------------------|
B |---------------------------|
G |---------------------------|
D |-----------------0--2------|
A |----2--0--2----------------|
E |---------------------------|
```

CONTINUED ON NEXT PAGE

Although this phrase has only five different notes, it contains enough to develop a larger idea. Try altering the pitch of one of the notes:

Variation 1

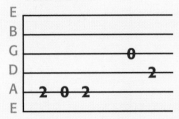

Now you have some variations to combine with the original motif:

Variation 2

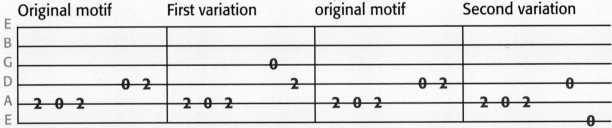

Original motif	First variation	Repetition of original motif	Second variation

You can also make a motif longer by adding notes to the beginning or end, creating a more rhythmically interesting line.

Variation 2B

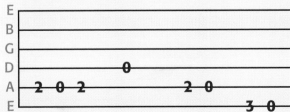

If you change the second variation, you get what is shown here.

```
     Original motif    First variation    Original motif    Second variation extended
E
B
G                            0
D              0  2              2              0  2           0
A    2  0  2        2  0  2        2  0  2        2  0  2    2  0
E                                                                 3  0
```

Try taking the repetition of the original melody and turning the direction around from a different place.

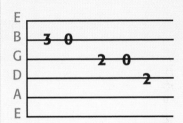

```
E
B    3  0
G        2  0
D            2
A
E
```

Now you have a longer, more complex melody that was originally created from a simple five-note motif. The four phrases—the original motif and its three variations—have enough similar features to make them seem related, but enough differences to keep them interesting.

```
     Original motif    First variation    Third variation    Second variation
E
B                                        3  0
G                            0              2  0
D              0  2              2              2              0
A    2  0  2        2  0  2                      2  0  2    2  0
E                                                                 3  0
```

chapter **15**

Advanced Techniques

You've learned the basics of improvising; now try some different techniques in your solos. Slides, pull-offs and hammer-ons, vibrato and string bending, and muting can all add more personality to your playing.

Sliding your finger from note to note gives your playing a more violin-like, liquid sound. It can make your guitar sound less percussive and more melodic.

How to Play a Slide

Instead of using different fingers of your fretting hand to play different notes, you can slide your finger from note to note on the same string. Here's one way of playing these two notes:

```
E
B    3        5
G
D
A
E
```

Your first finger plays the D on the 3rd fret (a) and your third finger plays the E on the 5th fret (b). You would pick both strings individually.

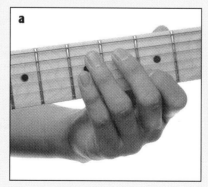

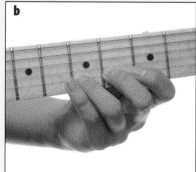

Now try this version:

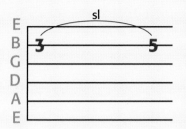

In this example, you pick only the D on the 3rd string and then slide your first finger to the 5th fret. The "sl" indicates that you slide between the 3rd (a) and 5th (b) frets, and only the first of the two notes is picked.

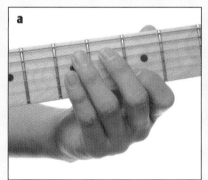

To make sure the sound doesn't fade away before you get to the 5th fret, use sufficient downward pressure on the string. You may also wish to pick the first note closer to the bridge to get sufficient punch in the pick stroke.

CONTINUED ON NEXT PAGE

Here's a longer passage involving multiple slides up and down the neck.

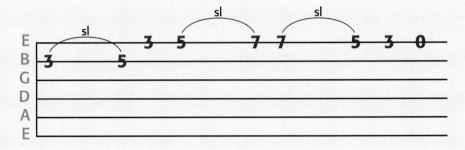

TIP

You can use slides in between notes if your phrase sounds too stiff or percussive. Sliding can give a guitar melody a more vocal, singing quality. Using several slides on the same string can also give the guitar a more tonally consistant sound, since every string has a slightly different tone quality.

Pull-offs and hammer-ons also allow a more fluid sound, where the fretting hand creates the sound on the string with some additional force. This makes some passages easier to play since you don't have to pick as many notes.

Pull-Off to Open Strings

Let's try a pull-off. The pull-off uses the fretting hand to sound a string.

```
E ———————— po ——— 0 ——————
B ——————————————————————————
G ——————————————————————————
D ——————————————————————————
A ——————————————————————————
E ——————————————————————————
```

Place your third finger on the 3rd fret of the High E string (a). Without using your picking hand, pluck the High E string with your third finger by pulling it toward the floor (b). You are essentially fingerpicking by using a finger on your fretting hand. The symbol "po" on the tablature refers to a pull-off.

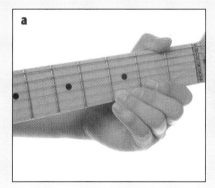

a

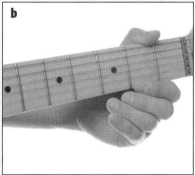

b

CONTINUED ON NEXT PAGE

Now use your picking hand to play the note on the 3rd string, and then again pull off to the open string.

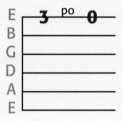

Pick the 3rd fret of the High E string (a).

Pull off with the third finger (b).

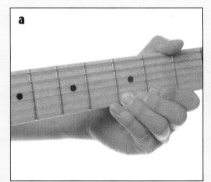

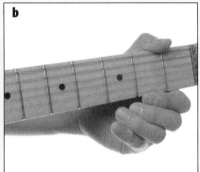

Try a series of pull-offs on the same string, but pull off from the 3rd fret, then the 5th, 7th, and finally back on the 5th, all going to the open string.

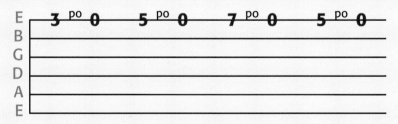

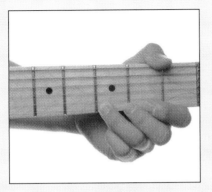

Pick 3rd fret of High E string

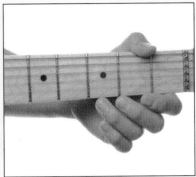

Pull off with third finger

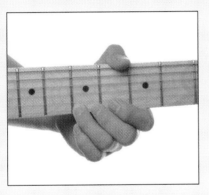

Pick 5th fret of High E string

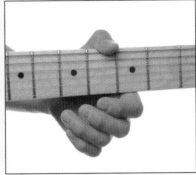

Pull off with third finger

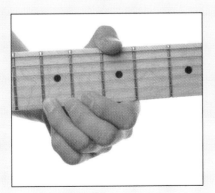

Pick 7th fret of High E string

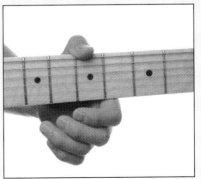

Pull off with third finger

CONTINUED ON NEXT PAGE

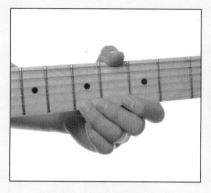

Pick 5th fret of High E string

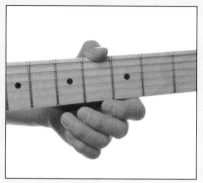

Pull off with third finger

Pull off to Fretted Notes

You can also pull off to other fretted notes, not just to open strings. In this example, the fourth finger pulls off after the note on the 8th fret is picked. However, the first finger is placed on the 5th fret before the pull-off.

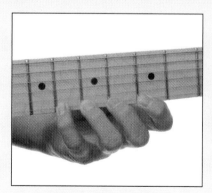

Pick 8th fret of High E string

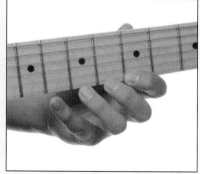

*Pull off with fourth finger to
5th fret of High E string*

Now let's try a series of pull-offs that go from the High E string, to the B string, and finally the G string.

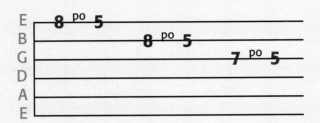

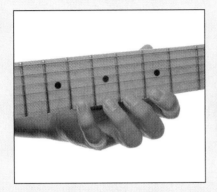

Pick 8th fret of High E string

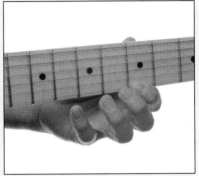

Pull off with fourth finger to 5th fret

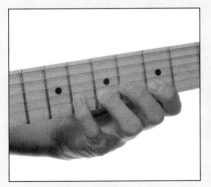

Pick 7th fret of the B string

Pull off with third finger to 5th fret

CONTINUED ON NEXT PAGE

Pick 7th fret of G string

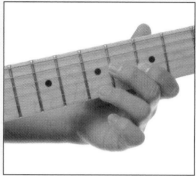

Pull off with third finger to 5th fret

Do a Hammer-On

The hammer-on is the opposite technique of the pull-off. Pick the open E string. Next, without using your picking hand, quickly and forcefully bring down the third finger of your fretting hand on the 3rd fret of the High E string. The force of your third finger, along with the momentum of the first picked note, should be enough to make the second note ring. The "h" in the tablature refers to the hammer-on.

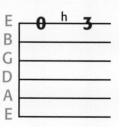

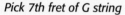

Pick open E

Hammer on with third finger
to 5th fret

Now try a series of hammer-ons on the same string, all starting from the open string.

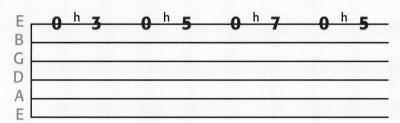

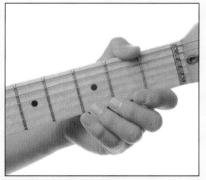

Pick open High E string

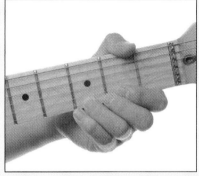

Hammer on to 3rd fret of High E string

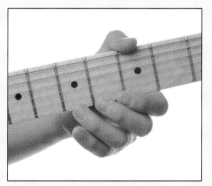

Pick open High E string

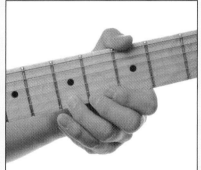

Hammer on to 5th fret of High E string

CONTINUED ON NEXT PAGE

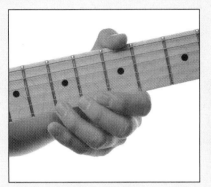

Pick open High E string

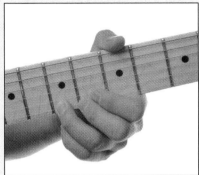

Hammer on to 7th fret of High E string

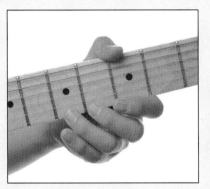

Pick open High E string

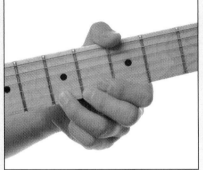

Hammer on to 5th fret of High E string

The hammer-on and the pull-off can be used together to create a seamless, violin-like sound.

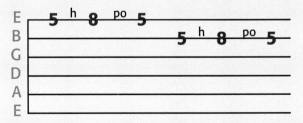

Pick 5th fret of High E string

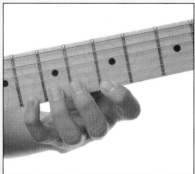

Hammer on to the 8th fret of the High E string

Pull off to the 5th fret of the High E string

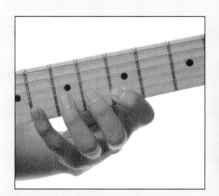

Pick 5th fret of High B string

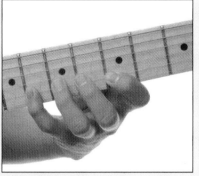

Hammer on to the 8th fret of the B string

Pull off to the 5th fret of the B string

Vibrato and String Bending

To give a guitar note a singing, vocal quality, you use a technique known as *vibrato*, where the pitch is slightly moved back and forth to create a singing quality like a human voice. *String bending* uses the same techniques as vibrato, but you're bending to a different note from where you start the bend.

Types of Vibrato

Vibrato involves a modulation of pitch created by moving the string. There are two basic types of vibrato:

Classical vibrato involves moving a left-hand fingertip back and forth along the string length, causing the string to tighten and loosen slightly, which causes the pitch to move. Classical vibrato is easier to apply to nylon-string guitars than to steel-string or electric guitars because the nylon-string tension is lower. This vibrato makes the pitch both rise and fall above the original note.

Vertical vibrato involves moving the string back and forth in a motion parallel to the frets. This vibrato is used in popular guitar styles, such as blues and rock. The pitch only rises compared to the original note.

CLASSICAL VIBRATO

1 Place your left-hand fingertip directly behind the fret of the note to be played and strike the string with your right hand (a).

2 Slowly rock and rotate the fingertip toward the fret. This causes the string to slacken slightly and the pitch to drop (b).

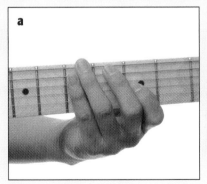

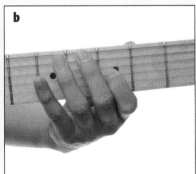

③ Slowly rock and rotate the fingertip away from the fret (see photo). This causes the string to tighten slightly and the pitch to rise.

Repeat moving the fingertip back and forth at a faster tempo. The faster you move your fingertip, the quicker the vibrato. As the note fades, slow the tempo of the vibrato until the fingertip is in its original position.

VERTICAL VIBRATO

① Let's use the third finger as an example. Place the left-hand third fingertip directly behind the fret of the note to be played. Place the first and second fingertips directly behind the third fingertip to lend extra muscle support. Place your thumb above the neck to be used as a fulcrum point, and strike the string with your right hand (a).

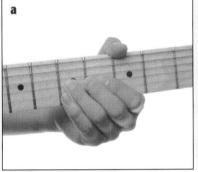

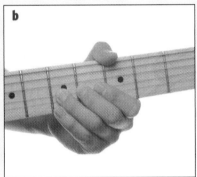

② Slowly push the third finger toward the thumb, using your first two fingers to help push. This causes the string to tighten slightly and the pitch to rise. When you relax your fingers, the string will pull to its starting position, and the pitch returns to the starting pitch (b).

③ Slowly pull the third finger away from the thumb, using your first two fingers to help pull (see photo). This causes the string to tighten slightly and the pitch to rise. When you relax your fingers, the string will pull to its starting position, and the pitch returns to the starting pitch.

Repeat moving the fingertip back and forth by continuing to push and pull at a faster tempo. The faster you move your fingertip, the quicker the vibrato. As the note fades, slow the tempo of the vibrato until the fingertip is in its original position.

CONTINUED ON NEXT PAGE

String Bending

The vibrato technique can also be used for string bending, where you move to a different note.

1 First play these two notes.

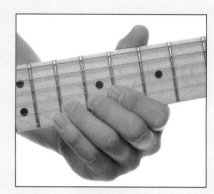

2 Now instead of playing the two notes separately, play the note at the 10th fret and then bend it up to the 11th. Make sure the pitch of the bent note is the same as the 11th fret note. The "b" in the tablature refers to a bend.

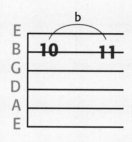

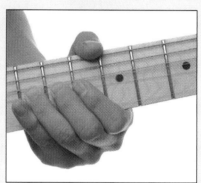

TIP

Bend slowly when you start, so you can make sure you're accurately hitting your target pitch.

You can also try bending two frets. First play:

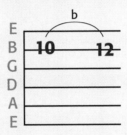

Then try bending the 10th fret up to the pitch of the 12th.

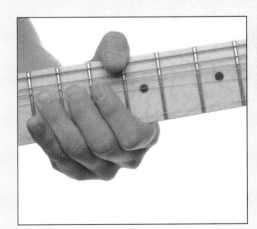

Once you reach your destination pitch, you can also apply vibrato, but be patient because these techniques involve specific muscle strength and memory.

All of these techniques can make a guitar sound more expressive and versatile. Try the examples presented in this chapter, which use all of the above techniques.

chapter 16

Purchasing and Maintaining Equipment

With the variety of manufacturers and options available, buying your first guitar can be confusing. That's why it's important to consider several factors before you buy.

Once you own a guitar, you need to know how to take care of it. Some of these tasks can done by you at home, while others will require expert attention.

Buying Your First Acoustic Guitar

Because acoustic guitar prices vary greatly, there are some factors to consider before purchasing a guitar, including budget. The main consideration, however, should be the instrument's playability and your attraction to its sound.

Trust Knowledgeable Friends and Instincts

Since you look down on the side of the guitar while you're playing, you're hearing only part of the sound. Bring a friend to a music store and have him or her listen to you play. Ask your friend to listen to you in different parts of a room, and also in different rooms. Also, have your friend play and listen to the sound as you walk around the room. You should be comfortable with both the sound of the guitar from both the player's perspective and the listener's perspective.

Even though it helps to do as much research as possible, remember that playing a musical instrument has to be a labor of love. Don't be surprised if you're drawn to an instrument you thought you'd never like. Conversely, don't think you'll grow to love an instrument that's a good deal, but has only a slightly attractive sound to you. Let your ears and instinct be the final judge.

Budget Considerations

Most high-end guitars are comprised of solid pieces of high-quality woods, including maple, rosewood, and ebony. Less expensive models are made of laminated or composite woods. A solid-top guitar is usually considered a better-sounding instrument, and it will often sound better over the years as the wood ages (see photo). You should expect to spend up to $400–$500 for a well-crafted, inexpensive model, but let your ears be the final judge. One of my favorite guitars has a solid wood top and laminate back and sides; it cost less than $350.

A laminated-top guitar is less likely to warp than a solid-top guitar because of the multiple levels of wood and the lacquer surrounding them.

Many newer guitars are made of composite wood, which are less expensive to produce. Composite wood guitars are not as rich in tones as solid wood guitars made of one type of wood.

CONTINUED ON NEXT PAGE

Styles of Acoustic Guitars

STEEL-STRING GUITARS

Steel-string guitars are used in blues, rock, and pop music. Both nylon- and steel-string guitars can be used in folk and country music as well. This is an ideal instrument for songwriting and accompanying singers.

NYLON-STRING GUITARS

Nylon-string guitars are the only guitars used in classical and flamenco music. They are also used in jazz and Brazilian music. If this is the type of music you intend to play, you will want to buy a nylon-string guitar.

Some beginners will choose to play the nylon-string guitar over the steel-string guitar because the nylon

strings are softer to the touch, especially to the beginner still building callouses. However, the nylon-string neck is slightly wider than the steel-string neck.

If you have extremely large hands or fingers, you may want to try a nylon-string guitar. Most nylon-string guitars have wider spacing between the strings to accommodate the classical technique, often referred to as "Segovia Technique" after famed classical guitarist Andrés Segovia, where the junction of the skin and the nail is used to pluck the string.

Buying Used or Renting

Buying a used guitar can be a great value, and many vintage instruments are prized for their tone and collectibility. However, beware of buying a used guitar that may cost a lot to repair later.

Renting a guitar is a viable option if you're not sure how much money you want to spend or what kind of guitar you want. However, they may be harder to play, or not sound quite as nice as other guitars, which might be discouraging. It's important that you understand how much of your early struggles are due to your lack of experience versus the instrument's problems.

A rental may be harder to play if the store hasn't had the time to adjust the action (see Tip below). It's important for a beginner to play on a guitar that's properly set up so that the player isn't working harder than necessary to play the instrument.

TIP

If the strings seem to be so high above the neck that it makes it hard for the fingers to press down, the guitar is considered to have high action. If the action is high, ask a sales person to adjust it. Make sure you're completely comfortable with the way a guitar plays before you purchase it.

Buying Your First Electric Guitar

The electric guitar offers more factors to consider. The type of body construction varies even more than in acoustic guitars, and the electronics and pickups also alter the way the strings are heard.

Body Construction

The most common body type for modern electric guitars is the solid body. Les Paul developed the first prototypes of his namesake solid-body guitars in the 1950s. Leo Fender headed up a parallel development of solid-body guitars. These guitars are great for modern applications of rock, country, blues, and pop. They have a present and punchy tone and will not feed back under normal situations.

Some guitars, such as the Gibson Les Paul, are made of several layers of different types of solid wood.

Other guitars, such as the Fender Telecaster, are made of one piece of wood.

Solid-body guitars are less susceptible to amplifier feedback. They are generally less expensive than their semi-hollow counterparts.

Semi-hollow guitars, such as the Gibson ES-335, have a solid block of wood running down the middle of the instrument, while the sides of the guitar are hollow. This design produces a sound that is punchy but still has some acoustic depth.

Pickups

The *pickup* is a specially designed microphonic device that delivers the sound of the string to the amplifier, without most of the incidental noise. The two most common pickups are the single-coil pickup and the humbucker pickup. A single-coil pickup has a clear, bell-like tone and is great for modern applications of rock, country, blues, and pop.

Most of the traditional Fender-style guitars, such as the Telecaster and Stratocaster, have single-coil pick-ups. In the following photos, the Telecaster is shown on the left; the Stratocaster on the right.

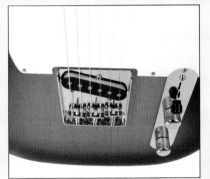

The humbucker pickup was developed to combat noise that the single-coil pickup often encounters. The humbucker is essentially two single-coil pickups wound together with wire. The interaction of the two coils magnetically cancels out noise and electronic hum, hence the name "humbucker." These pickups have a broader sound with more emphasis in the midrange. If you're planning on playing rock, heavy blues, or jazz, this might be the pickup for you.

Buying Your First Amplifier

The electric guitar and the amplifier work as a team to shape the final sound. The type of amp and the electronic options it offers can drastically change the sound of the guitar and how it functions in any musical genre.

Tube Amplifiers

The most important factor in how an amp sounds is whether the sound of the electric guitar is being amplified on older vacuum-tube technology or more recent solid-state technology. Tube amplifiers generally sound warmer and feel more touch-sensitive than solid-state amplifiers. However, they also require more maintenance. Tubes will eventually need to be replaced, and you will occasionally need to have a service professional adjust the voltage settings.

Solid-State Amplifiers

Solid-state amplifiers are often more affordable than tube amplifiers and do not have to be serviced. They are not usually thought to have the same richness in sound as tube amps, but solid-state amps have been improving steadily over the years. Newer models often incorporate modeling technology, which enables them to imitate any number of sounds, replicating older amps and effects. However, if they break, they're often hard to fix.

Effects like distortion, reverb, vibrato, chorus, and delay are common in modern amps. Newer amps also can utilize modeling technology, which allows the amp to imitate a variety of different types of amplifiers from different eras.

Care and Maintenance of Your Strings

Taking care of your strings can prolong their lifespan. By doing so, your strings will be able to retain their tonal clarity and their ability to stay in tune longer.

Prolong the Life of Your Strings

To make your strings last longer, wipe them down with a clean, dry cloth after you finish playing. This prevents sweat and dirt from oxidizing on the string.

There are other things you can do to prolong the life of your strings. Excessive heat, cold, and humidity can reduce a string's life span. Avoid keeping the guitar in the trunk of your car during extreme weather. Also, some people need to change their strings more often because of the acidity of their hand sweat.

When to Change Your Strings

In time, sweat and dirt from your hands will start to tarnish and dull the guitar strings. Eventually, the high-end brilliance and low-end bass frequencies suffer. The guitar sounds less vibrant and full. The instrument also does not ring as long.

A guitar with old strings is also harder to tune. The string eventually becomes fatigued from the constant pressure of being stretched across the guitar. Here are some tuning problems you may encounter:

- You may constantly need to retune certain strings.

- Some strings may seem to be in tune for one chord, but out of tune for others.

In any of these situations, you should change the strings.

FAQ

Is there an average life span of a guitar string? Six months? One year?

Absolutely not. I change strings every 6 days. My other professional friends can go months.

Although strings can physically last for years, you'll notice an improvement in sound quality if you change strings every 2 to 3 months.

How to Restring Your Guitar

You should change your guitar strings whenever the tone or tuning suffers. Here's how to restring quickly and easily and keep your strings in tune.

How to Restring Steel-String Acoustic Guitars

1 Start by removing the old string. You'll see that one end of the guitar string is held in place by ball ends, which are placed in the holes of the bridge, and held in place by the bridge pins. If you can't remove the bridge pins manually, use a string winder, which has a notch you can use to pry the pin out.

2 Once you've removed the bridge pin, place the new string back in the hole. Replace the pin so the groove in the pin faces the nut. The pressure of tuning the string up to pitch will keep the bridge pin in place. Keep light pressure on the pin if it shifts (see photo).

3 Your next step is to fasten the strings at the tuners. First reserve a certain string length that will wrap around the tuners. Assume that about two inches of string will be needed beyond where the string reaches each tuner. Bend that string as a reference point and thread it through the tuner, so the string is turned around the top of the tuner.

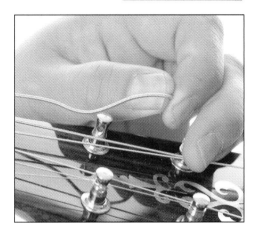

4 Thread the string through the hole of the tuner.

5 As you hold the string taut with your left hand, slowly wind the tuner so the tension on the string increases. The first wrap of the string should be above the string length you are holding. After the first wrap is complete, the rest of the windings should be underneath the string length, and should continue winding downward. It's important to wrap the string neatly. Tangles and odd windings will eventually shift as you play.

6 The first wrap of the string should be above the original string length (a). Subsequent wraps should be below the original string length and continue downward (b).

CONTINUED ON NEXT PAGE

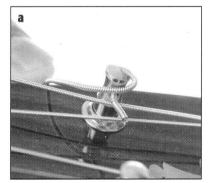

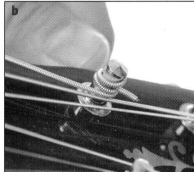

7 While tuning the string up to pitch, you may wish to pull on the string at the twelfth fret to let the string stretch. This stops the string from stretching out while you are actually playing. It also prevents tangled windings while you turn the tuners.

Note: Even more so than with steel strings, you have to stretch out nylon strings before you start playing.

How to Restring Nylon-String Guitars

BALL END STRINGS

Some nylon-string guitars use strings that have ball ends similar to steel strings. In those cases, simply place the string through the bridge, then wind the other end of the string through the tuners, as described in "How to Restring Steel-String Acoustic Guitars," step 4.

SPECIAL TIES

Classical or flamenco nylon-string guitars require a special tie to fasten the string. Once the string is placed through the end, it should be brought back up and wrapped around the top of the string. Then the remaining string length is wrapped around the original length toward the bottom of the bridge.

How to Restring Electric Guitars

Electric guitars are strung in a similar manner as acoustic guitars, but you thread the ball end through a metal bridge piece. Some guitars, such as the Fender Telecaster (a) and Stratocaster, allow the strings to pass through the bridge saddle all the way through the body (b).

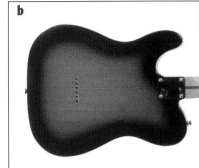

Other guitars, such as the Les Paul, have tailpieces on the top of the guitar where the string starts.

Others have a moveable bridge where the pitch of the strings can be lowered by depressing a moveable arm, known as a tremolo bar.

The other end of the string is fastened to the tuners in the same way described in "How to Restring a Steel-String Acoustic Guitar," Step 5.

The Truss Rod

It's important to have your guitar set up so it's both easy to play and free from buzzing.

What Is the Truss Rod?

Steel-string and electric guitars have a steel rod inside the neck called a truss rod. The end of the truss rod is adjusted using a hex wrench. The end of the truss rod can be found either at the top of the headstock underneath a cover or simply within a hole, or where the neck meets the body inside the guitar.

The truss rod controls how much the neck bends. The neck must have a slight bend or the strings will buzz when pressed down. Nylon-string guitars and older or less expensive steel-string guitars will not have a truss rod.

The truss rod needs to be adjusted seasonally, as weather and humidity shift.

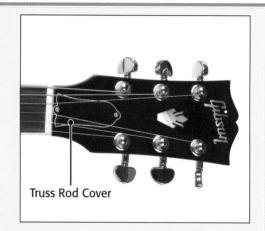

Truss Rod Cover

Let the Pro Fix the Truss Rod for Now

If the neck is too flat, the strings will buzz, especially if it is played with a lot of dynamics. However, you don't want the guitar strings so high that it's uncomfortable or infeasible for your fingers to push the strings down, especially if you're playing barre chords or chords that use the pinky of your fretting hand. These adjustments should initially be done by a guitar repair professional, to make sure there are no other issues, and so that you have to perform only safe and simple maintenance tasks at home.

Again, the following procedure should be left to a professional for now; but here's how to do it when you know your way around the guitar a bit more. If the strings are buzzing excessively, especially on the first six frets, the truss rod may be too tight. Loosen it by turning the truss rod wrench counterclockwise, no more than an eighth of a turn each time. If the strings are too high, especially around the twelfth fret, the truss rod may be too loose. Tighten it by turning the truss rod wrench clockwise, but again, no more than an eighth of a turn each time.

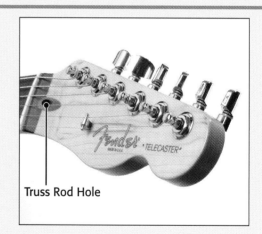

Truss Rod Hole

Don't tighten the truss rod too hard, because excessive pressure could cause it to break. Replacing a truss rod is an expensive procedure. Let the guitar sit overnight before making another adjustment; it may take awhile for the truss-rod adjustment to show. If the problem does not resolve itself, take the guitar to a repair professional.

If your electric guitar doesn't seem to be in tune consistently across the neck (fretting sharp or flat to what they should be), it may be intonated improperly. Here's an easy way to adjust the intonation of the guitar with just an electronic tuner and a Phillips screwdriver.

How to Adjust the Intonation

TUNE OPEN STRINGS FIRST

Note: *Before you intonate your guitar, make sure you start with a fresh set of strings. You may have to re-intonate the guitar if you use a different gauge of strings or change the height of the bridge.*

For each string, hit the open string and use your electronic tuner to tune it. Now play the 12th fret, which is the same note, one octave up. If the 12th fret note is exactly the same according to your tuner, that string is properly intonated.

TUNE THE 12TH FRET OF THE SAME STRING

If the note on the 12th fret is flatter (lower in pitch) than the open string, use the screwdriver to turn the screw on the saddle the string rests on so it moves forward. This raises the pitch of the twelfth note relative to the open string. If the note on the 12th fret is sharper (higher in pitch) than the open string, use the screwdriver to turn the screw on the saddle the string rests on so it moves backward. This lowers the pitch of the twelfth note relative to the open string. After each screwdriver adjustment, retune the open string using the tuner, and then recheck the twelfth fret note. Repeat this procedure until both notes are in tune.

Humidification

Dry air can dry out your guitar, causing damage to its structure and finish. Luckily it's easy to care for the instrument with a few humidification tips.

Keep Your Guitar from Drying Out

When cold temperatures set in, it's easy for the wood in your guitar to dry out without additional moisture. Low humidity can cause cracking to both the finish and the wood of the guitar.

If you are not returning your guitar to its case after playing, you should use a room humidifier. Even better is placing the guitar in its case with a small guitar humidifier in the sound-hole. A small amount of water injected into the soundhole will be released in a controlled manner.

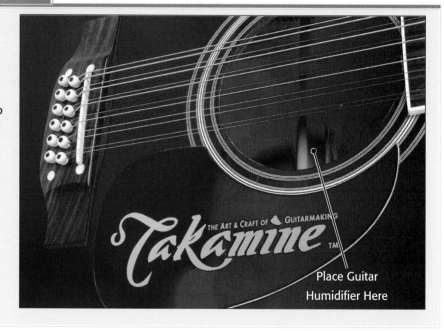

Place Guitar Humidifier Here

Here are some other procedures you should let a professional handle.

Go to a Professional for These Jobs	
Problem	*What's wrong*
The body underneath the bridge is swollen and curved, pushing the strings away from the fingerboard.	Excessive dryness has caused the wood to warp.
The first several frets are too high to play.	The nut and/or the action may need to be adjusted.
The volume/tone controls make a scratchy noise through the amp when moved.	The control pots are dirty and need to be cleaned.
The strings rattle and fret out when played.	The action needs to be adjusted.
The bridge on your suspension bridge keeps rising when you try to tune the guitar.	There is not enough tension holding the bridge in place and it needs to be adjusted.

chapter **17**

Electric Guitar Sounds

While the electric guitar has the same tuning and fingerboard layout as an acoustic guitar, its sound can be manipulated in ways an acoustic guitar can't. This chapter discusses controls on the guitar, the amplifier, and effect processing.

A note on digital effects and amp simulation: With the advent of digital technology, many modern amps can mimic a variety of vintage amps and effects using virtual modeling technology. A player can select a sound that resembles a small tube amp, a medium-size solid-state amp, or a 100-watt amp-and-speaker combination.

Some amps can also add the sounds of delays, reverbs, choruses, and other pedal processors (see "Effect Pedals") that are usually purchased separately.

Controls on Your Electric Guitar

The volume control, tone control, and pickup selectors on your guitar enable you to change the sound leaving the guitar before it gets to your amplifier.

Volume Control

The volume control affects the volume output that leaves the guitar. Some guitars, such as the Fender Stratocaster (a) and the Telecaster (b), have one master output. You have only one knob to turn, even if you are using more than one pickup at the same time.

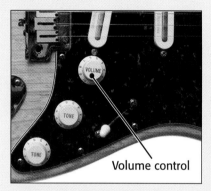

Volume control

Volume control

Note: *In many guitars, as you turn the volume down, you may hear an incidental drop in the treble frequencies of the guitar. One guitar that doesn't have this problem is the Telecaster, which has an extra capacitor in the wiring.*

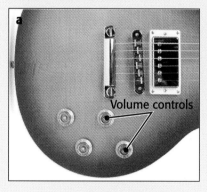

Volume controls

Volume controls

Other guitars, such as the Les Paul (a) and the Gibson SG (b), have a control assigned to each pickup.

Tone Control

Most tone control affects the treble or high-end content of the guitar's tone. When the tone control is turned all the way up, the sound of the guitar is unaltered. As you turn the knob, the sound of the guitar will become darker and less trebly. Many guitarists who play jazz, blues, or ballads will do this to get a warmer, more horn-like sound. Pictured here is the ES-335 tone control.

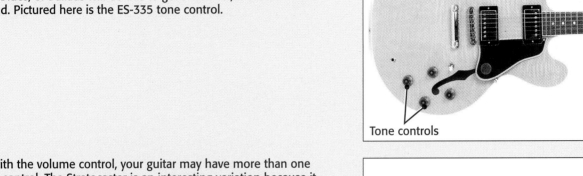

Tone controls

As with the volume control, your guitar may have more than one tone control. The Stratocaster is an interesting variation because it has a tone control for each pickup except the rear pickup. The tone is then controlled by the treble control on an amplifier.

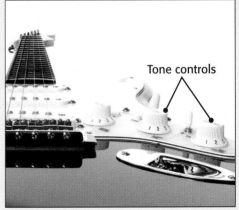

Tone controls

TIP

While most tone control simply removes high-end content, guitars with active electronics can add or subtract a variety of frequencies. Active electronics require some type of power source, usually a 9-volt battery inside the guitar itself.

Controls on Your Amplifier

The amplifier controls are the last factors you can control before the electric guitar sound hits your ears. Let's investigate how the amplifier's volume, tone, reverb, and other controls affect the sound of the guitar.

Volume Control

ONE MASTER CONTROL

Some traditional amps, such as the Fender Twin amp, have only one master volume control that makes the volume of the amplifier louder or softer.

MASTER CONTROL PLUS OVERDRIVE

Newer amps, however, may have a master volume, plus a secondary overdrive, distortion, or gain control to create a distorted sound. First, you use the overdrive/gain knob to control how much distortion you want. Then you slowly turn the master volume control up until you reach the desired playing volume.

DUAL CHANNEL

More advanced amplifiers might have two sets of volume controls: one for a traditional clean, undistorted sound, and one for overdriven sounds.

Tone, Reverb, and Tremolo Control

Tone control on an amplifier typically consists of treble, midrange (or "mid"), and bass controls. Some amplifiers may also have a presence knob or a bright switch, which allows for even brighter frequency control than a traditional treble control.

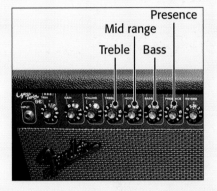

Presence
Mid range
Treble | Bass

Your amp may have a reverb control, which simulates a cavernous sound, as if you were playing in a large amphitheater or hall.

Note: *Traditionally, control of the reverb was done with electric circuitry leading to a small metal tank with vibrating springs in the back of the amplifier. Modern amps can also do this with digital simulation .*

Reverb knob

Another common feature is a set of controls for tremolo. This allows for an undulating or wobbling change of the guitar's intensity. The controls are usually labeled "intensity" (how strong the tremolo's pulse is), and "speed" (how fast the pulse moves). Reverb and tremolo used together was a common staple of 50s and 60s surf music.

Intensity
Speed

Effect Pedals

By using effect pedals, you can alter the sound of your guitar and add electronic color, enhancing the possibilities of what the guitar can do alone.

The most common pedal for many players involves overdrive, distortion, or fuzz. All of these effects involve changing the gain structure of the electric guitar's sound.

Overdrive, Distortion, and Fuzz

OVERDRIVE

Overdrive is the most subtle of the effects. The sound of overdrive simulates the sound of a tube amplifier when it's turned louder. It allows the player to have a more sustained sound, plus a crunchier edge. An overdrive pedal is a convenient way to switch between sounds quickly, by turning the pedal on and off between overdriven and clean sounds. Overdrive is used by rock, blues, and pop players.

DISTORTION

Distortion is a grainier, more intense sound than overdrive, and even further removed from the sound of the original electric guitar tone. There is more sustain and higher levels of gain produced. Distortion is used by players of hard rock, heavy metal, punk, and alternative music.

FUZZ

Fuzz is a more extreme version of distortion. The fuzz pedal is fatter and less subtle than either overdrive or distortion. Fuzz also adds a lot of extra noise to the sound of the guitar, so players must mute the strings not played or they may start feeding back. Many 60s rock icons (think Jimi Hendrix or Jeff Beck with the Yardbirds) favored these pedals.

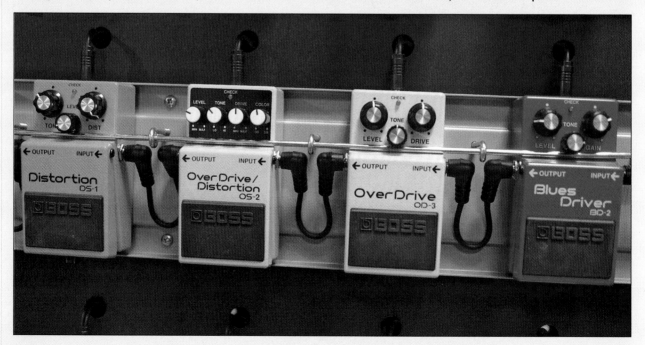

DELAY AND REVERB PEDALS

These pedals take the sound of the original guitar and make a copy of the sound that repeats after the first sound is heard.

The delay pedal allows one or more echoes to be heard after you play a note. A delay with a short time is called a slapback. Many early rock and rockabilly records use slapback echoes on guitar and vocals to create a punchy echo. Longer echoes can be used to create intertwining sounds that give the illusion of multiple guitar players.

The reverb pedal is similar to the delay pedal, but uses many delayed signals to approximate the sound of the guitar echoing in a large room such as a concert hall or theater. This pedal can also be used in conjunction with amps that do not have their own reverb controls.

VOLUME PEDAL

The volume pedal does the same as the volume knob on your guitar, but enables you to leave both hands free to play the guitar because your foot controls the volume. The pedal is based on a rocker mechanism that turns a control. When your heel depresses the pedal, the guitar's volume is completely turned off. When you press your toe down, the guitar's volume is fully turned on. You can use the pedal to control the output of the guitar by moving the pedal up and down while you play. If you leave the pedal in the down position (sound completely off) and then hit the string, the guitar sounds like a bowed violin when you press your toe on the pedal.

WAH-WAH PEDAL

The wah-wah (or "wah") pedal looks like a volume pedal, but the control changes a boost in tone. As you move your foot over the rocker mechanism from heel to toe, the sound of the guitar swells from a bassier tone to a more trebly tone, imitating the sound of a human voice.

chapter **18**

Continuing Your Guitar Education

Now that you've started your musical journey with the guitar, you'll want to find ways to pursue your playing. Here are some options to consider as you use this book as a reference.

Use a Private Teacher

Now that you've worked on some of the basics, you might seek the guidance of a private instructor. With a teacher, you can work on individual playing issues and specialize in different types of music.

Benefits of Private Instruction

Nothing can replace the inspiration and clarity that come by working with a professional musician. Use this book as a resource while your teacher helps you focus on specific playing issues. He or she can work with you to design a special program of songs, exercises, and skills to take your playing to the next level of proficiency.

> **TIP**
>
> Make sure you're clear on what your teacher expects from you in terms of both short-term and long-term development. That way you will know how to realistically gage your progress, and can spare yourself unnecessary frustration.

Learning music theory can help you understand the interaction of melody, harmony, and rhythm. Although a complete knowledge of music theory is not essential to simply play a song, it can open up many possibilities, such as improvising, composing, and arranging music, and figuring out songs by yourself.

Benefits of Studying Music Theory

Music theory is the study of scales, chords, and rhythm. You may be surprised to learn that you have been introduced to many elements of music theory in this book. By continuing to study music theory, you can eliminate some of the memorization that's involved with playing the guitar by learning general rules that can be applied in all songs.

A knowledge of theory is also a powerful tool to use in improvising, composing, and writing songs or music for the guitar. Music theory is not a substitute for musical creativity, but can make musical understanding and communication easier.

Learn from Other Guitarists

Part of the beauty of music is the interaction and sharing you experience when playing with others. Learn from your friends as you use your guitar as an outlet for musical communication.

Make Learning a Shared Thing

Continue the learning experience by playing with other musicians who are slightly more experienced than you are. You'll gain guidance and inspiration, as well as ideas about what to pursue in your independent studies or with your instructor.

Also, play with friends who are beginning guitarists like you. Realize that some of your friends might learn certain things faster than you; however, don't worry about it or compare yourself negatively to them. Every guitarist finds certain tasks easier than others. Your neighbor may find it easy to play barre chords, but may find it hard to play finger-style guitar as well as you do. Everyone's development differs from skill to skill.

Remember to set realistic goals for yourself. Don't set your standards so high that if you don't meet them you get discouraged and give up. Muscle strength and muscle memory doesn't develop overnight, but will eventually develop with consistent practice.

PRACTICE, PRACTICE, PRACTICE!

As I mentioned in Chapter 1, practice is most effective when it is regular and consistent. A half hour a day is better than cramming a four-hour session once a week. Muscles and reflexes need a regimen to stay sharp. If you know you won't be able to practice every day, then try to play every other day. If you're taking lessons, try to practice a little right after you meet with your instructor. Doing so provides a great chance to ingrain what you have learned while it is fresh in your mind.

WORK ON DIFFERENT SKILLS

As you continue to learn new skills, including different fretting techniques, lead guitar, and different rhythmic approaches, you may find that certain musical skills are harder

to master than others. Don't let work in one area stop you from working on skills in other areas. For example, don't feel that you have to master barre chords before you experiment with lead guitar. You may find you have a knack for vibrato and string bending, but your index finger muscle may still need to develop some strength to perform these skills competently.

Finally, don't forget to have fun! Don't let technical goals obscure the reason you picked the guitar.

Chord Charts

Here's a compilation of many of the chords taught in this book. As you get more adept at your playing, you can use this appendix as a quick, at-a-glance reference for many of the common chords you will encounter. For information about how to read a chord chart, see Chapter 5, "Your First Chords."

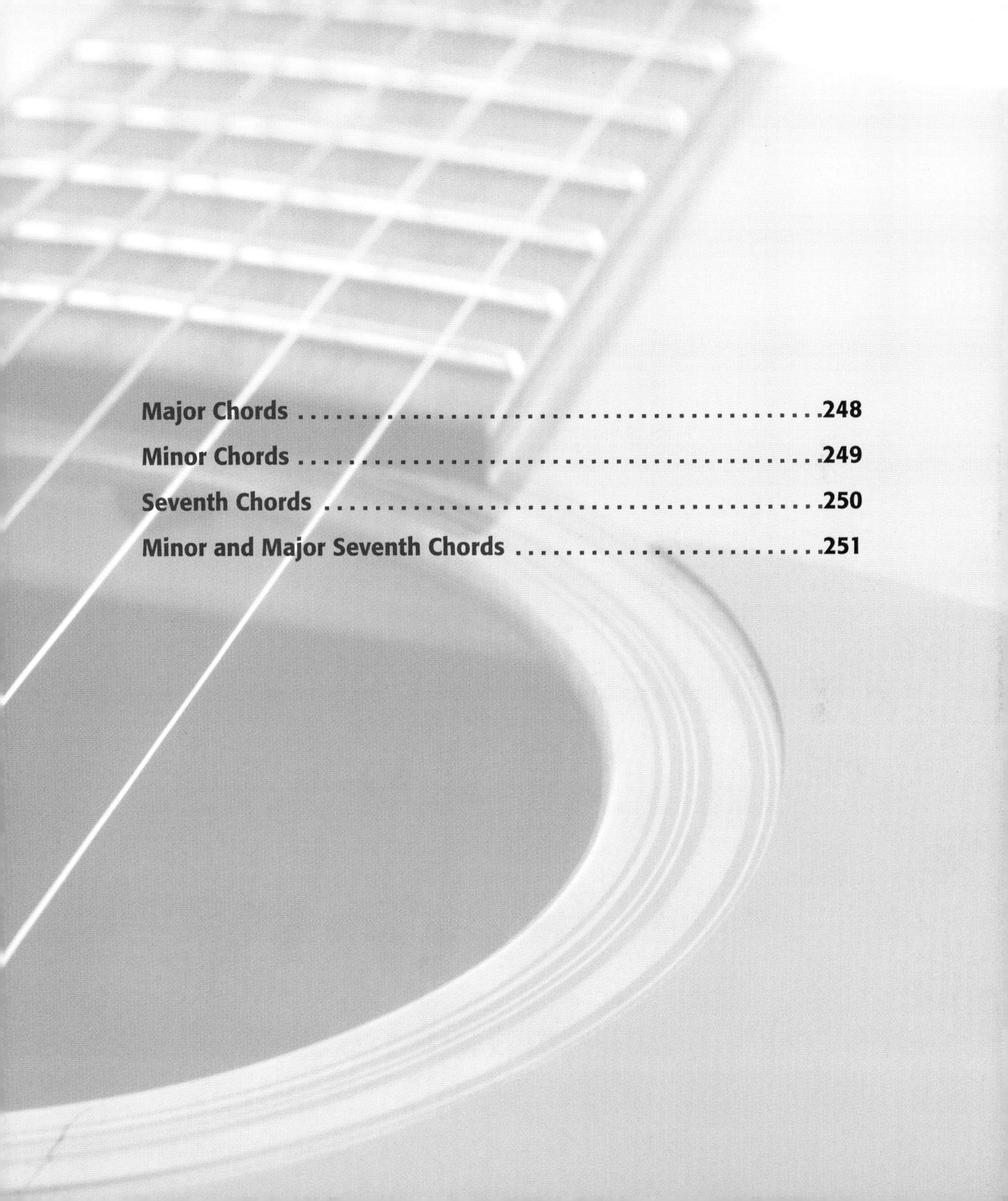

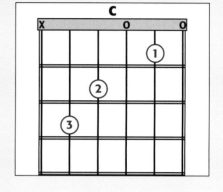

A

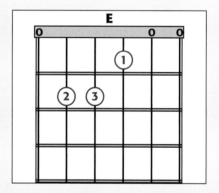

C

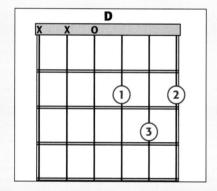

D

E

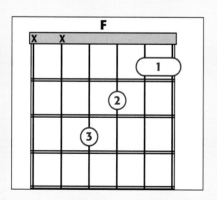

F

G

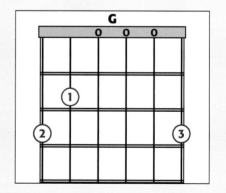

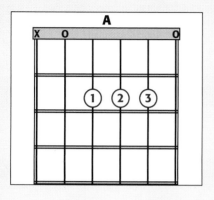

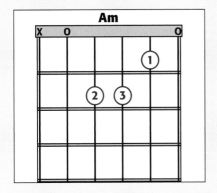

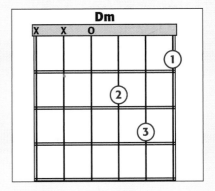

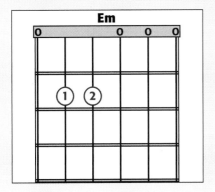

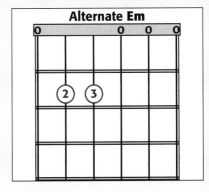

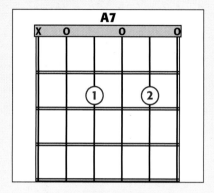

A7

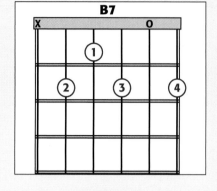

B7

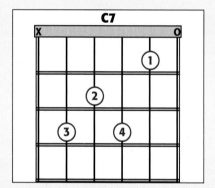

C7

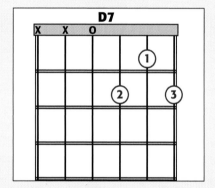

D7

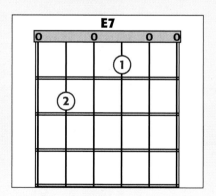

E7

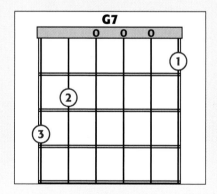

G7

Minor and Major Seventh Chords

MINOR SEVENTH CHORDS

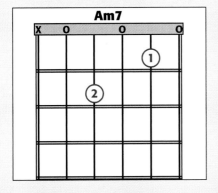

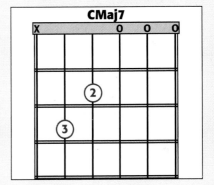

MAJOR SEVENTH CHORDS

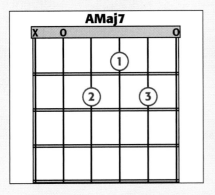

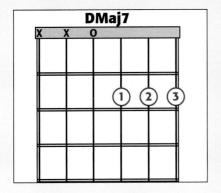

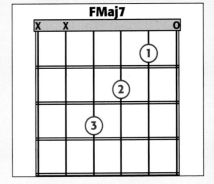

appendix B

Scales

This appendix includes tablature for several basic scales that you can use while warming up and practicing. Although playing scales is often not as much fun as playing songs, scales are important for dexterity and musical knowledge, and understanding and practicing them will enable you to master more complex and accomplished pieces. The root notes in each scale are circled.

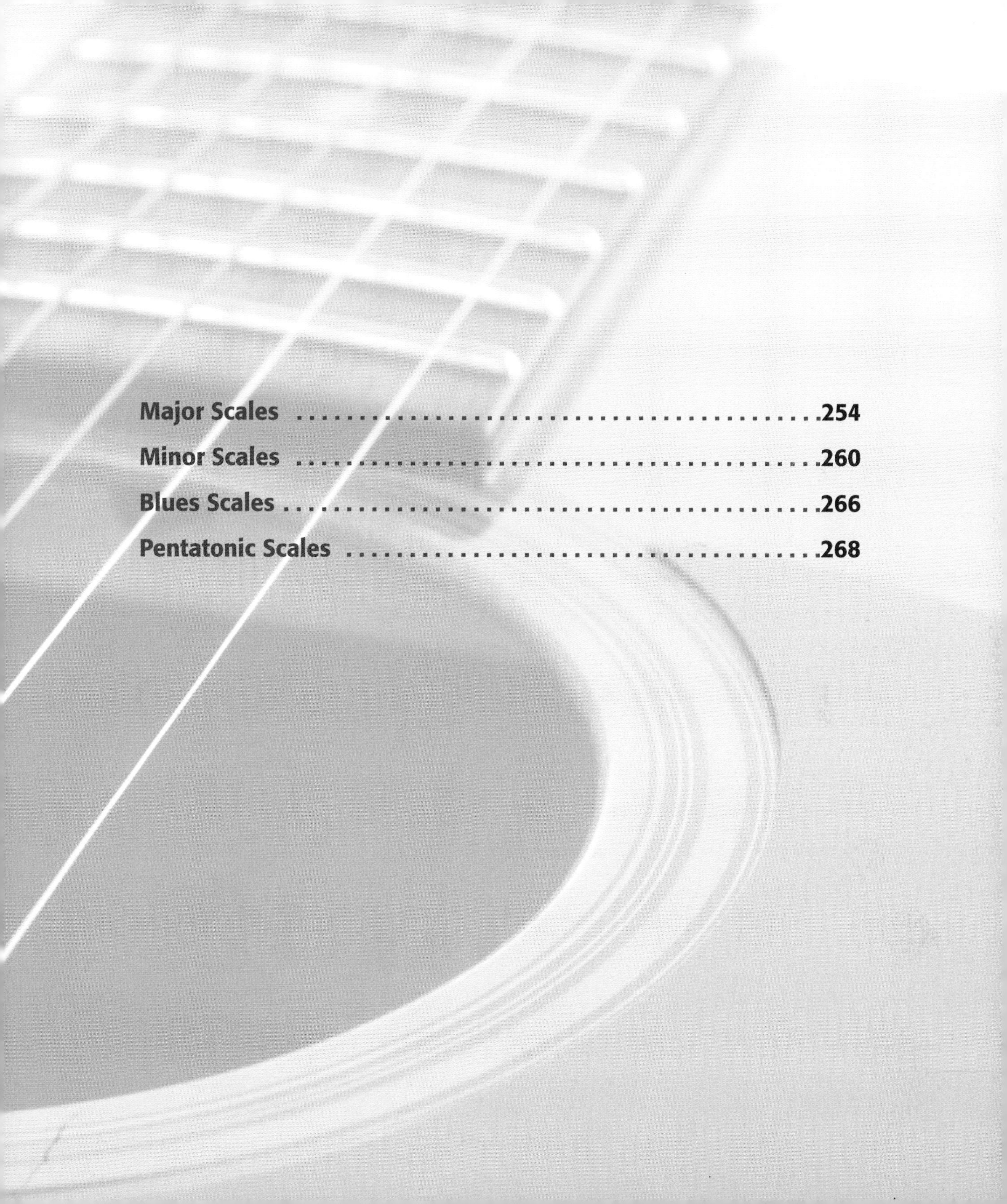

C MAJOR

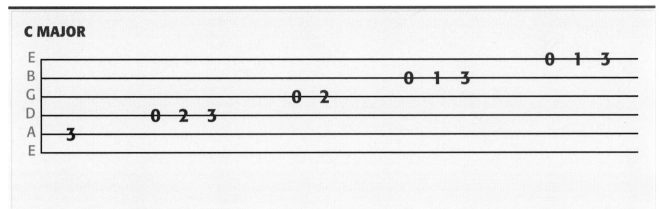

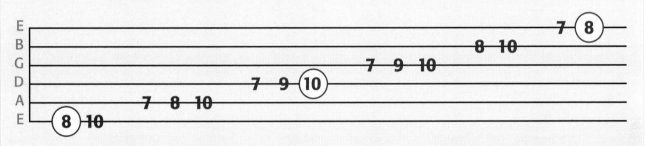

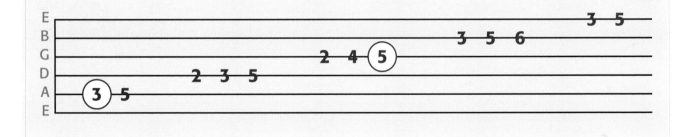

D MAJOR

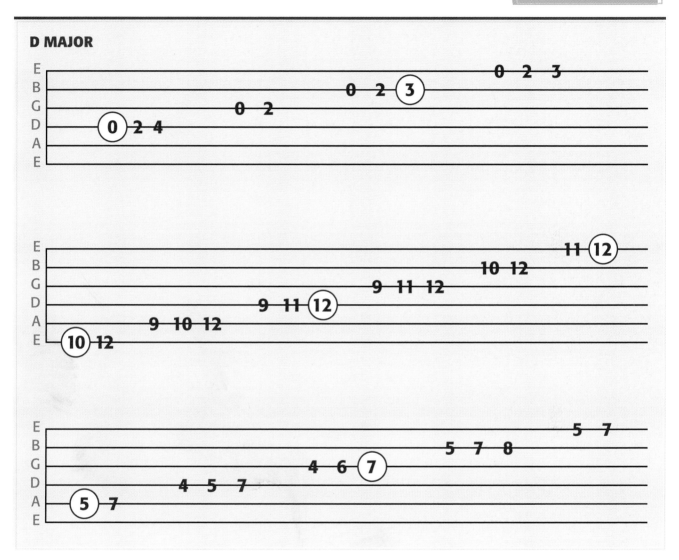

CONTINUED ON NEXT PAGE

E MAJOR

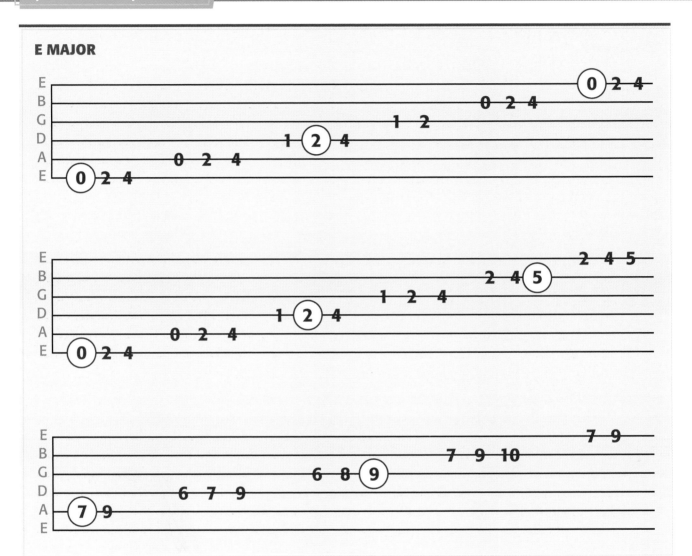

F MAJOR

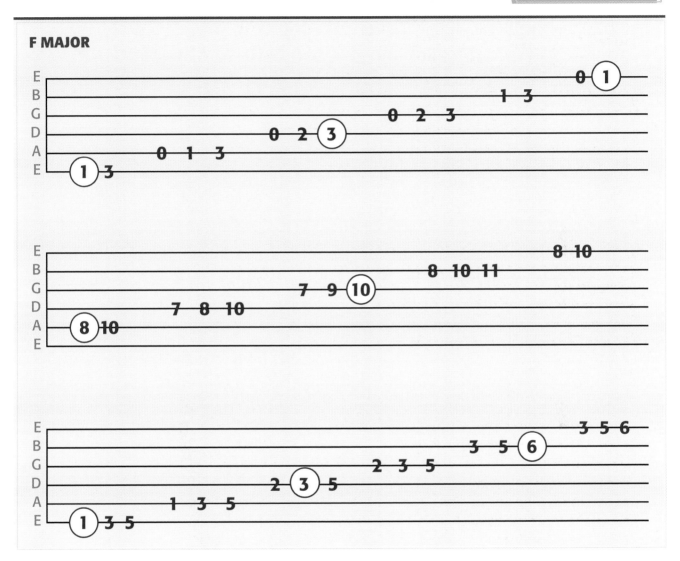

CONTINUED ON NEXT PAGE

G MAJOR

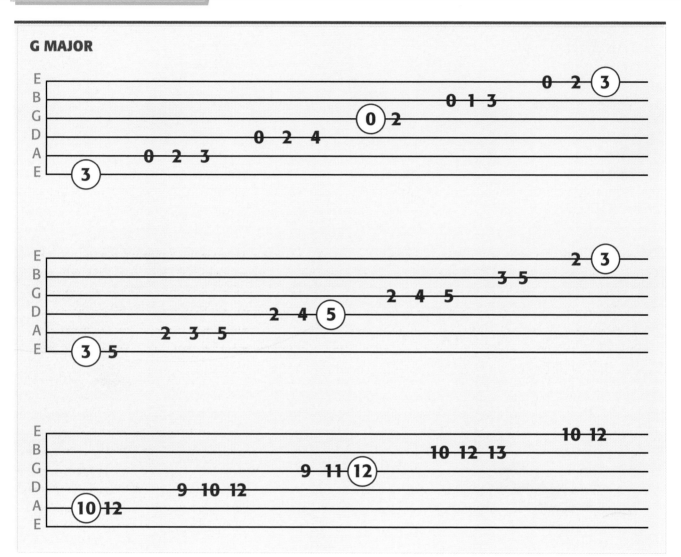

A MAJOR

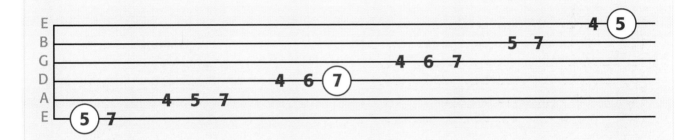

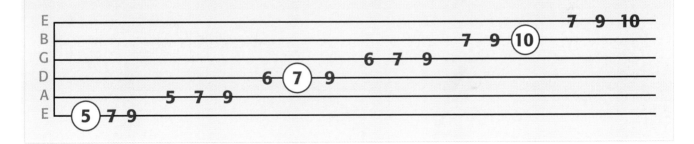

A MINOR

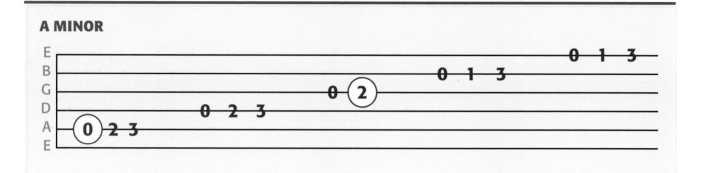

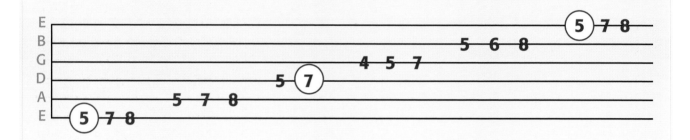

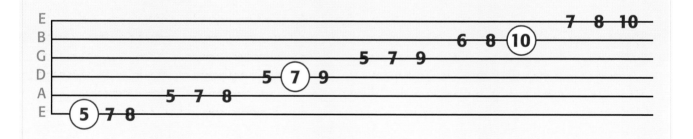

B MINOR

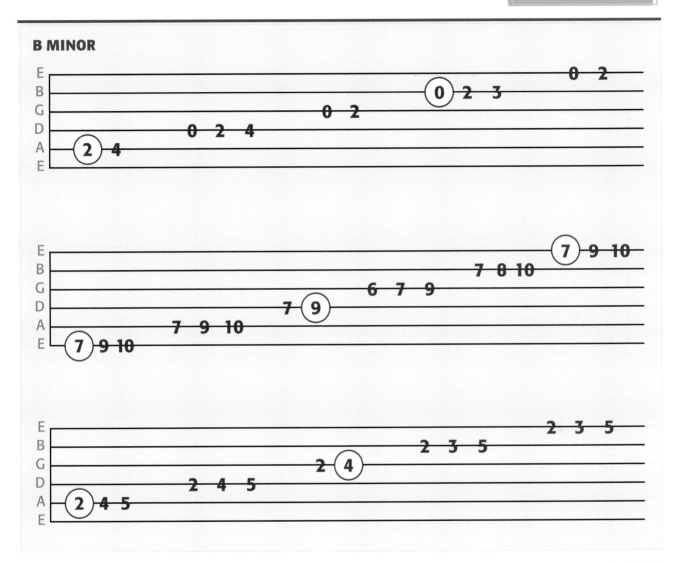

CONTINUED ON NEXT PAGE

C# MINOR

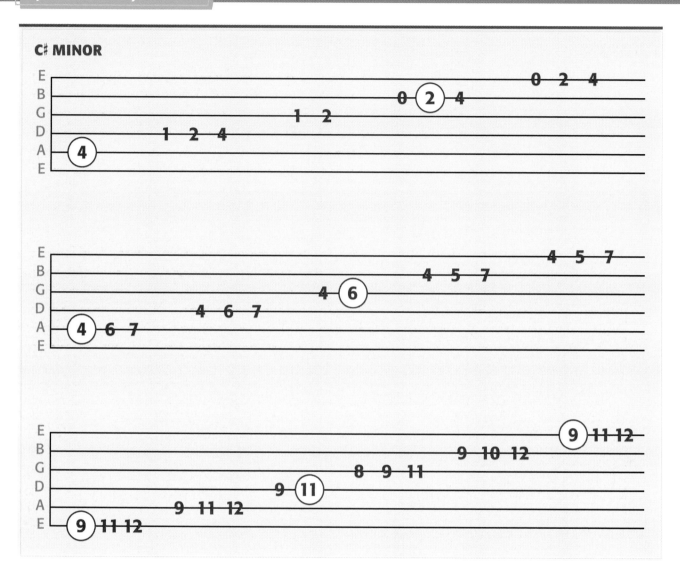

D MINOR

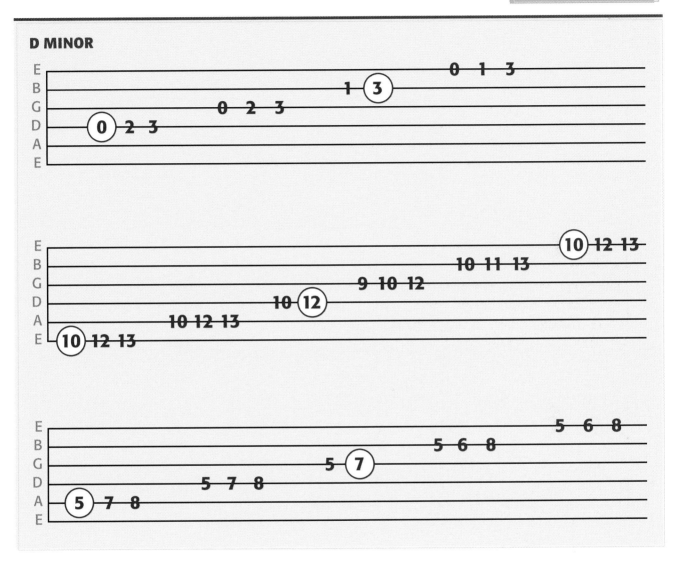

CONTINUED ON NEXT PAGE

E MINOR

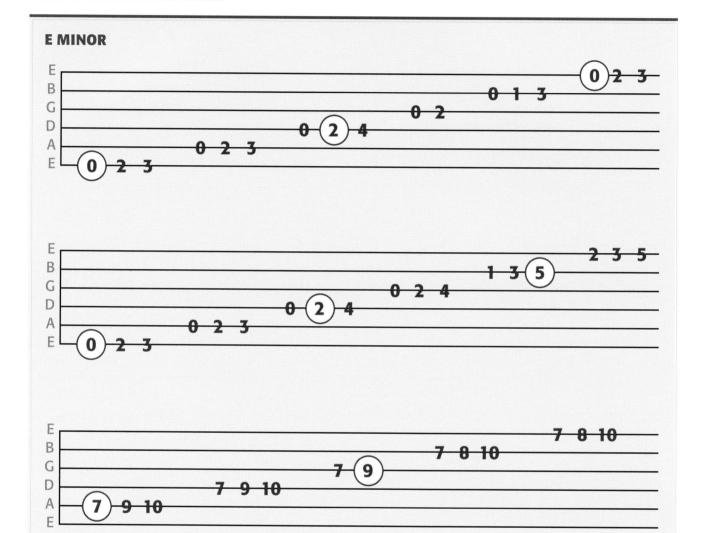

F# MINOR

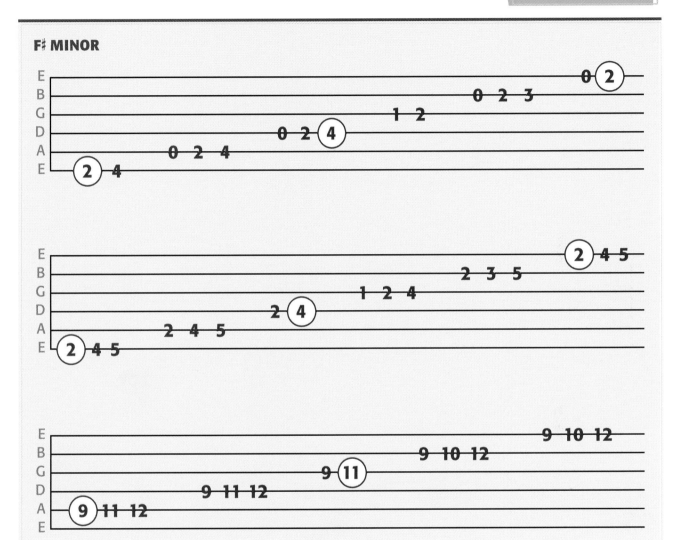

A BLUES SCALE

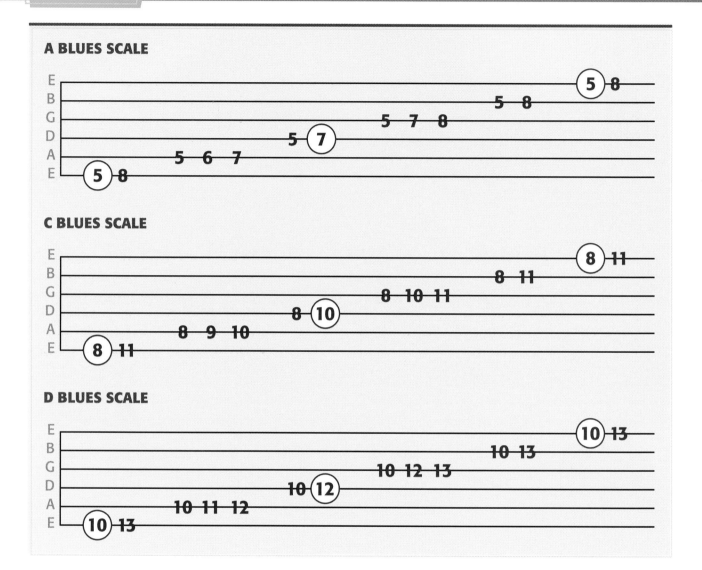

C BLUES SCALE

D BLUES SCALE

G BLUES SCALE

E BLUES SCALE

Pentatonic Scales

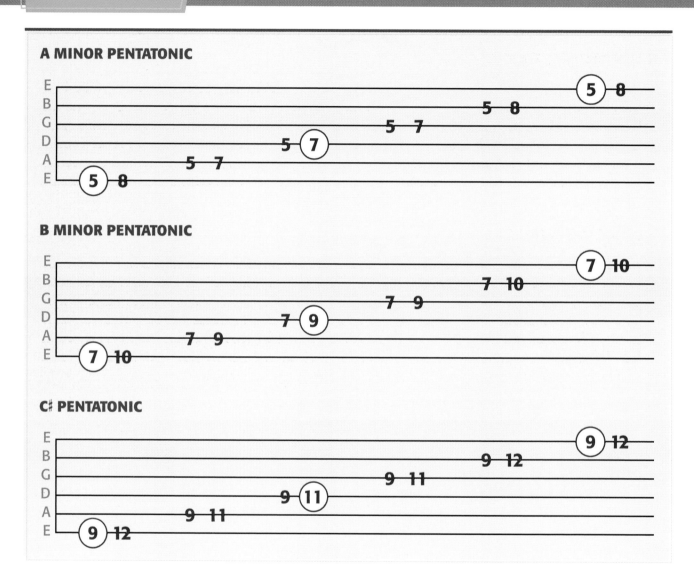

A MINOR PENTATONIC

B MINOR PENTATONIC

C♯ PENTATONIC

D MINOR PENTATONIC

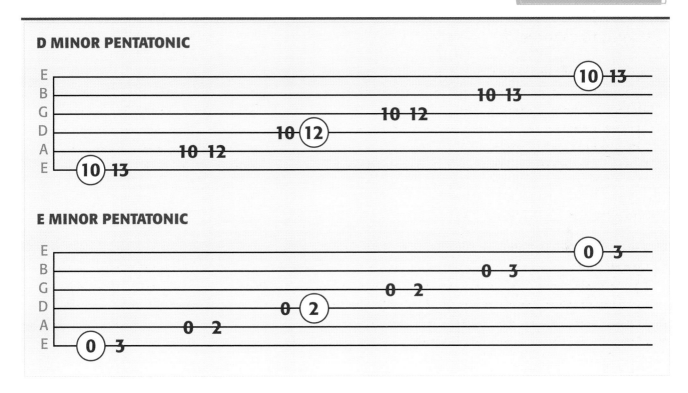

E MINOR PENTATONIC

appendix C

Guitar Gallery

The pages that follow show some popular acoustic and electric guitars. When shopping for a new guitar, you'll find that your options are nearly limitless. Before purchasing, be sure to visit several music stores in your area and ask the salespeople lots of questions. Sample a variety of guitars and play the ones you're most interested in extensively before making your final decision. You want to find the guitar that fits you best.

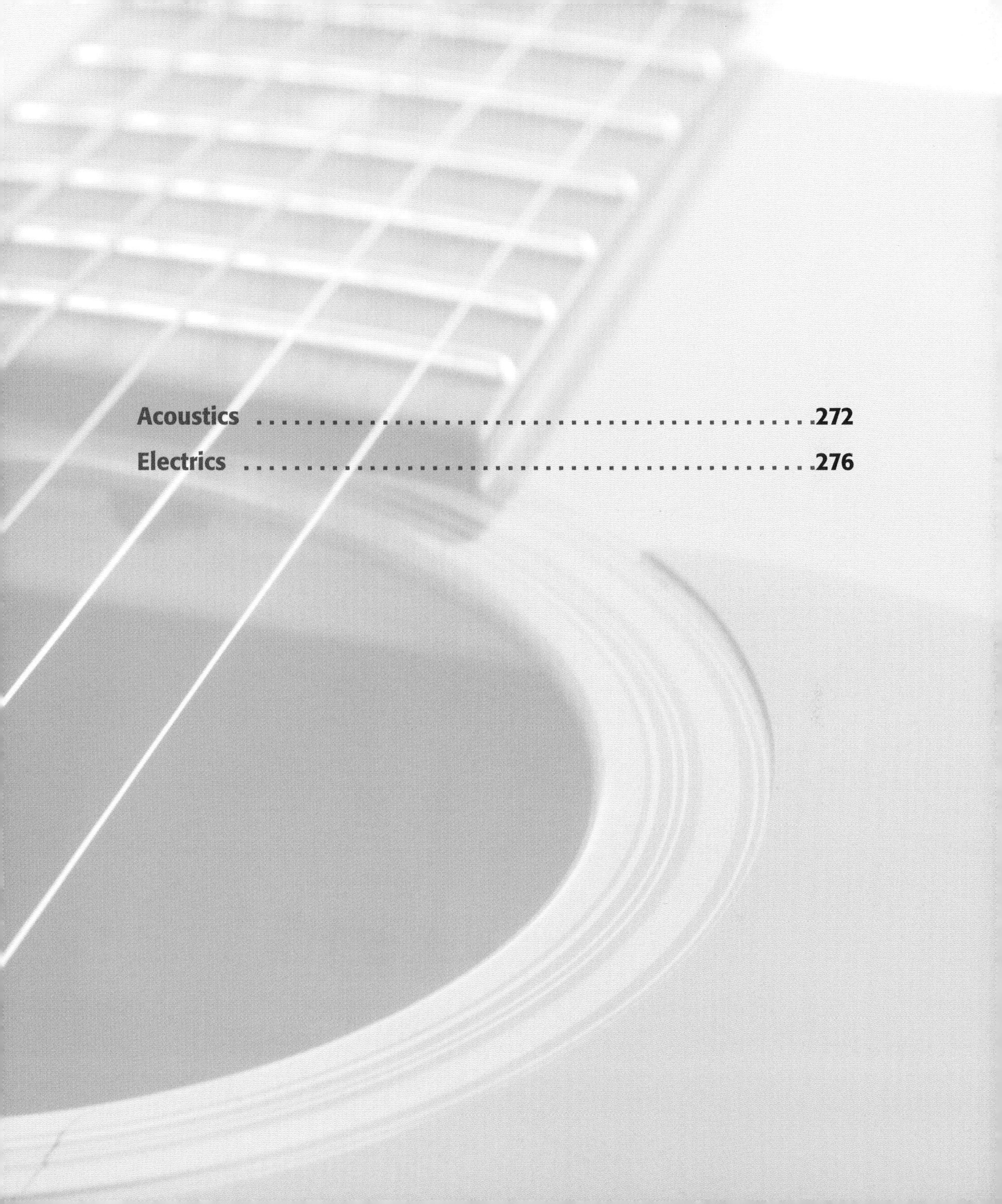

FENDER DG-22S

GUILD GAD-40

GIBSON HUMMINGBIRD

TAKAMINE EF-381C

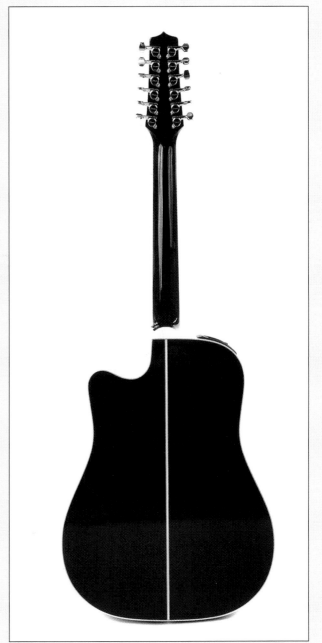

FENDER STRATOCASTER

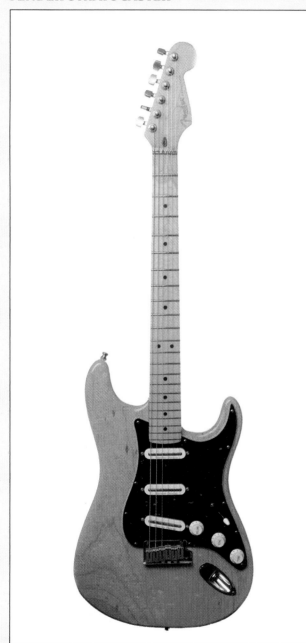

FENDER TELECASTER

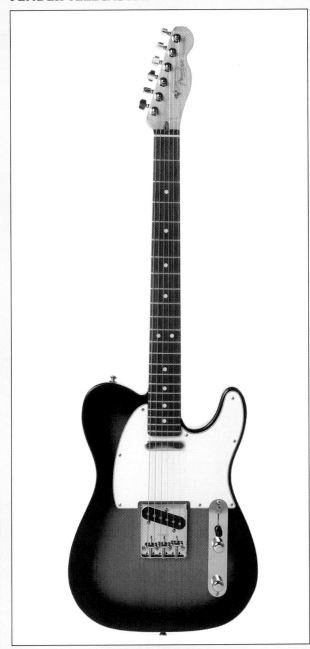
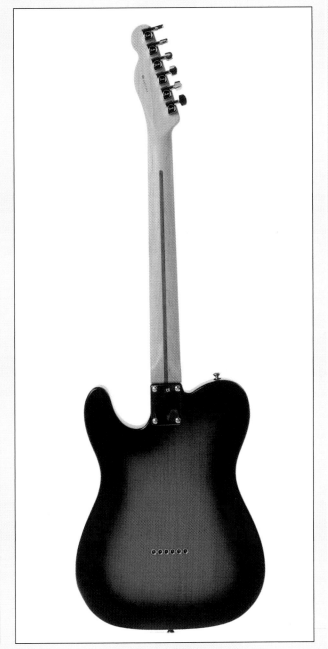

GIBSON LES PAUL

GIBSON ES-335

GIBSON SG

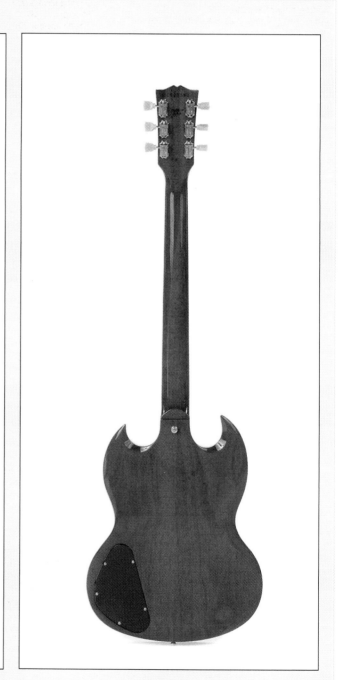

Index

Numbers

3/4 strumming patterns, 87
4/4 strumming patterns. **See also** rhythm guitar; strumming
    down strums, 85
    playing, 84–85
    prominent downbeats, removing, 86
    up strokes, removing, 85
4/4 time signature, 83

A

A7 chord, 60, 91, 136, 159
A7sus2 suspension, 136
A7sus4 suspension, 136
A blues scale, 190
A chord
    capo use, 159
    chord chart, 90, 135
    fingering, 90
    strum, 75
A string
    in chord chart, 56
    illustrated, 26
    relative tuning, 32, 33
    tuning, 30, 31
acoustic guitars, 272–275
    budget considerations, 215
    laminated-top, 215
    parts illustration, 10
    purchasing, 214–217
    restringing, 224–226
    styles, 216
    tuning pegs, 12
    used/renting, 217
active electronics, 235
advanced techniques
    hammer-ons, 204–207
    pull-offs, 199–204
    slides, 196
    string bending, 210–211
    types of, 194
    vibrato, 208–209
affordability, 4
air guitar test
    sitting position, 42–43
    standing position, 48
Am7 chord, 94, 138, 159
Am7sus2 suspension, 138
Am7sus4 suspension, 138
Am chord, 93, 137, 159
AMaj7 chord, 92
amplifiers. **See also** electric guitars
    dual control, 236
    master control, 236
    master control plus overdrive, 236
    purchasing, 220–221
    reverb control, 237

    solid-state, 221
    sound additions, 232
    tone control, 237
    tremolo control, 237
    tube, 220
AMsus2 suspension, 137
AMsus4 suspension, 137
arpeggios, 77, 78–79
Asus2 suspension, 135
Asus4 suspension, 135

B

B7 chord, 95, 159
B string
    in chord chart, 56
    illustrated, 26
    relative tuning, 33, 34
    tuning, 30, 31
ball ends, 224, 227
barre chords. **See also** capo; chords
    A-based, chart, 173
    Bm, 169–173
    defined, 154
    E-shape, chart, 169
    F, 163–169
    muscle development, 162
    playing, 161–162
    technique, 161–162
    thumb position, 50
bass runs
    characteristics, 130
    defined, 150
    examples, 152–153
    exercise, 150–151
blues, chord progressions, 183
blues scale. **See also** pentatonic scales
    A, 190, 266
    C, 189, 266
    D, 266
    defined, 187
    E, 267
    G, 188, 267
    as moveable scale, 188
Bm barre chord. **See also** barre chords; chords
    B5, 172
    B7, 171
    B, 171
    beginner, 169–170
    Bm7, 172
    full, 171
    intermediate, 170
body, guitar
    acoustic guitar, 10
    defined, 15
    electric guitar, 11
    elements, 10, 11, 16
    illustrated, 10, 11, 15

bridge
    defined, 17
    Floyd Rose, 18
    illustrated, 10
    Les Paul, 17
    moveable, 227
    pins, 224
    steel-string, 17
    Stratocaster, 18
    Telecaster, 17
buying. **See** purchasing

C

C7 chord, 97, 160
C blues scale, 188
C chord, 96, 139, 160
C major pentatonic, 188
C minor pentatonic, 188
capo. **See also** barre chords
    chord changes with, 159–160
    defined, 156
    illustrated, 156
    placement, 156
    theory, 157
    using, 156–160
chord charts. **See also** chords
    major chords, 248
    minor chords, 249
    seventh chords, 250
    minor and major seventh chords, 251
chord progressions
    blues, 183
    common, 182–183
    folk, 182
    key and, 176
    rock, 183
    use of, 174
chord shifts. **See also** chords
    to adjacent string, 65
    with common fingering, 66
    without common string, 70–71
    D to A7, 67
    D to E7, 68–69
    economy of motion, 64–65
    finger movement, 70
    finger relaxation, 64
    G to Em, 66
    practice strategy, 71
    on same fret, 67
    on same string, 68–69
chords
    A7, 60, 91, 136, 159
    A, 75, 90, 135, 159
    Am7, 94, 138, 159
    Am, 93, 137, 159
    AMaj7, 92
    B7, 95, 159

goals, 6
Gsus4 suspension, 149

H

half-step, 157
hammer-ons
    defined, 204
    playing, 205–206
    with pull-offs, 206–207
    sound, 199
    technique, 204
hands
    in fretting position, 49–51
    instrument familiarity, 7
    in learning chords, 57
    training, 6
headstock
    acoustic guitar, 10
    defined, 12
    electric guitar, 11
heel, 14
humbucker pickups, 20, 219
humidification, 230

I

intonation adjustments, 229

K

keys
    figuring out, 176–177
    importance, 176
    major, 177, 178, 179
    minor, 180
    roman numerals for, 178–181

L

lead sheets
    bar lines, 122
    defined, 118
    illustrated, 118–119
    irregular chord shifts, 122
    patterns in, 122
    playing songs from, 118–123
Les Paul guitars, 17, 21, 227, 278

M

maintenance procedures, 231
major chords
    characteristic, 112
    identification, 112
    list of, 112
    seventh, 114
major keys
    list, 177
    pentatonic scales, 189

major scales, 254–263
markers, 13
melodies, creating, 191–193
memory, developing, 6
metronomes, 86
minor chords. *See also* chords;
    specific minor chords
        characteristic, 113
        list of, 113
        seventh, 115
        symbol, 113
minor keys
    list, 180
    pentatonic scales, 190
minor scales, 260–265
motifs
    defined, 191
    lengthening, 192
    melody creation with, 191–193
    variations, 192, 193
muscle strength, 6
music genres, 4
music theory, 243
muting, 77

N

neck
    acoustic guitar, 10
    correct viewing, setting position, 41
    electric guitar, 11
    elements, 13–14
nut, 14
nylon strings, 226
nylon-string guitars
    restringing, 226
    string spacing, 216
    use, 19, 216

O

output pack, 23
overdrive pedal, 238

P

pentatonic scales
    blues, 187–188
    C blues, 189
    C major, 188
    C minor, 188
    defined, 186
    E minor/G major, 186
    G blues, 188
    G minor, 187
    major key, 189, 268
    minor key, 190, 268, 269
    relative, 189
pick guard, 16

picking hand position
    finger brace, 53
    illustrated, 52
    pick use, 53
picking technique, 72–79
picks
    strumming with, 76–77
    use, 53
pickups
    guitar purchase and, 219
    humbucker, 20, 219
    illustrated, 11
    selector switch, 20
    single-coil, 20, 219
playing
    barre chords, 161–162
    with friends, 244
    hammer-ons, 205–206
    from lead sheets, 118–123
    singing and, 120
    slides, 196–198
    songs you like, 7
    starting/stopping, 7
power chord, 167, 172
practice
    chord shifts strategy, 71
    importance, 245
    regime, developing, 7
private instruction, 242
pull-offs
    to fretted notes, 202–203
    hammer-ons with, 206–207
    illustrated, 199, 200, 201, 202, 203
    to open strings, 199–202
    sound, 199
purchasing
    acoustic guitars, 214–217
    amplifiers, 220–221
    budget considerations, 215
    electric guitars, 218–219
    instincts and, 214
    used guitars, 217

R

relative major/minor scales, 189
relative tuning. *See also* tuning
    chart, 34
    defined, 32
    process, 32–33
renting guitars, 217
resolved chords, 177
restringing
    electric guitars, 227
    nylon-string guitars, 226
    steel-string acoustic guitars, 224–226
reverb control, 237
reverb pedal, 239

Teach Yourself VISUALLY™ books...

Whether you want to knit, sew, or crochet...strum a guitar or play the piano...train a dog or create a scrapbook...make the most of Windows XP or touch up your Photoshop CS2 skills, Teach Yourself VISUALLY books get you into action instead of bogging you down in lengthy instructions. All Teach Yourself VISUALLY books are written by experts on the subject and feature:

- Hundreds of color photos or screenshots that demonstrate each step or skill

- Step-by-step instructions accompanying each photo
- FAQs that answer common questions and suggest solutions to common problems
- Information about each skill clearly presented on a two- or four-page spread so you can learn by seeing and doing
- A design that makes it easy to review a particular topic

Look for Teach Yourself VISUALLY books to help you learn a variety of skills—all with the proven visual learning approaches you enjoyed in this book.

0-7645-9641-1

Teach Yourself VISUALLY™ Crocheting

Picture yourself crocheting accessories, garments, and great home décor items. It's a relaxing hobby, and this is the relaxing way to learn! This Visual guide *shows* you the basics, beginning with the tools and materials needed and the basic stitches, then progresses through following patterns, creating motifs and fun shapes, and finishing details. A variety of patterns gets you started, and more advanced patterns get you hooked!

0-7645-9640-3

Teach Yourself VISUALLY™ Knitting

Get yourself some yarn and needles and get clicking! This Visual guide *shows* you the basics of knitting—photo by photo and stitch by stitch. You begin with the basic knit and purl patterns and advance to bobbles, knots, cables, openwork, and finishing techniques—knitting as you go. With fun, innovative patterns from top designer Sharon Turner, you'll be creating masterpieces in no time!

0-7645-9642-X

Teach Yourself VISUALLY™ Guitar

Pick up this book and a guitar and start strumming! *Teach Yourself VISUALLY Guitar* shows you the basics photo by photo and note by note. You begin with essential chords and techniques and progress through suspensions, bass runs, hammer-ons, and barre chords. As you learn to read chord charts, tablature, and lead sheets, you can play any number of songs, from rock to folk to country. The chord chart and scale appendices are ready references for use long after you master the basics.

designed for visual learners like you!

0-7645-7927-4

Teach Yourself VISUALLY Windows XP, 2nd Edition

Clear step-by-step screenshots *show* you how to tackle more than 150 Windows XP tasks. Learn how to draw, fill, and edit shapes, set up and secure an Internet account, load images from a digital camera, copy tracks from music CDs, defragment your hard drive, and more.

0-7645-8840-0

Teach Yourself VISUALLY Photoshop CS2

Clear step-by-step screenshots *show* you how to tackle more than 150 Photoshop CS2 tasks. Learn how to import images from digital cameras, repair damaged photos, browse and sort images in Bridge, change image size and resolution, paint and draw with color, create duotone images, apply layer and filter effects, and more.

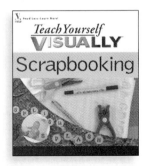

Available wherever books are sold.

Visual
An Imprint of ⊕**WILEY**
Now you know.